CANDY

True Tales of a 1st Cavalry Soldier
In the Korean War and Occupied Japan

By Kenneth J. LaRue

with William D. LaRue

COVER PHOTO: This book's author Kenneth J. LaRue, far left, stands with other members of George Company, 2nd Battalion, 8th Cavalry Regiment behind a hill along the front line in Korea in fall 1951, maybe just a quarter-mile from the enemy. At the top of that steep hill behind them were trenches where members of his company lived.

Dedication

This book is dedicated to my Korean War squad leader, Newton "Steve" Babcock, whose mix of friendliness and quiet confidence gave us a certain assurance that we would be okay.

— Kenneth J. LaRue

Table of Contents

Foreword

When I was about 8, my father, Kenneth James LaRue, pulled out an old wooden box and sat at our kitchen table. Dad took off the lid and pulled out all sorts of souvenirs that he collected in the Army during the Korean War. The contents included some ghastly photos of Chinese war dead, a black-and-yellow shoulder patch with a horse on it, several glistening medals, a map of Japan and a tiny notebook with lots of handwriting in pencil.

As he pulled out the items and described them, he told me a little bit about how he had served in combat against the North Korean enemy and its Chinese allies in late 1951.

Being a kid, my first question was, of course, "Did you get shot?"

"No."

"Did you kill anybody?"

My father kind of squirmed a bit, as I recall, and finally answered. "I don't know. I fired a lot of shots at the enemy. But they were kind of far away. It was hard to tell if I hit someone."

That was pretty much it. I hung around a few minutes until I got bored and wandered away as my father sat there with his box of memories. Soon, he put the lid back on and stored the box on a shelf to gather dust for a few more years.

Thank God he didn't throw it away.

Years later, after he retired, all of that material – from military documents to faded photographs to letters home to his parents – was a treasure trove in telling the story of my dad's experiences of going off to war.

Dad came from a village in Upstate New York. He served for three years in the U.S. Army, right after he graduated from high school. He received many military awards and honors, including the Combat Infantry Badge. But after he was honorably discharged in 1953, like a lot of Americans, he didn't think a whole lot about the Korean War. That was the past. He told me he focused his life on getting married, raising three children and making a living as an office worker.

After he retired in 1994, he finally had enough time to put his wartime experiences back where they belonged on the front shelf of his life. He joined various veterans groups and began reading more about the much vaunted 1st Cavalry Division, where most of his Army service occurred. He also spent hours talking with me about these experiences while I documented them on video. This is a story he wanted told.

At the persistent urging of my sister, Nancy, my father wrote out a basic summary of his wartime service. He diligently typed 11 single-spaced pages, a copy of which he gave to me for use in this book. Dad was a natural storyteller with a seemingly endless well of tales from before, during and after the war. What dates and names he couldn't recall off the top of his head, we usually found in paperwork and old photos in that wooden box.

.

My father smiles for a photograph in 2002. Although he was known to many as Kenny, he told me he hated that nickname and preferred instead to be called Ken.

As with many military memoirs, this book offers its share of battlefield horrors. But some of my father's best stories involved him and his buddies in off-duty horseplay straight out of an episode of "M*A*S*H," the quintessential Korean War farce. Dad more than anyone understood that this book at its heart would be a coming-of-age story about a young man finding his moral compass.

This book is not meant to be a detailed examination of the history and military strategy of the Korean War. There are many good books on those subjects. This book does find room, though, for Dad's thoughts on the war's Big Picture.

Dad suffered for years from heart disease and other medical

conditions, but he never displayed to me any obvious signs of post-traumatic stress disorder, which was known in his Korean War days as "shell shock." Then, about two months before he died, I was sleeping over at his home in Canton, New York, when I heard him scream, "Bill! Bill!"

I raced down the hall to his bedroom. He was sitting up, his head cupped in his hands. I never had seen my big, strong father looking so vulnerable.

"I'm sorry, I just had a panic attack," he told me. "I was dreaming I was back in Korea and I couldn't get home. I kept calling 911 but couldn't get an answer."

He said it was the first time he ever had any kind of flashback to Korea.

My father died November 30, 2012, at a nursing home in Massena, New York. He was 80 years old. While his body finally gave in to heart disease, his mind retained his intellect and devotion to family right to the end. The week he died he completed in shaky penmanship a Christmas list detailing the gifts to his children, grandchildren, brother and sister.

Not a day goes by that I don't long to talk to Dad again. I treasure our recorded conversations, bittersweet as they are to hear. Often when I edited a story in this book, my first reflex was to pick up the phone, call my father and make sure I didn't misunderstand something he told me. The fact that this is impossible is why readers should put the blame on me for any shortcomings in these pages.

Dad had a wonderful funeral, including a military salute at the grave site. Attached to his gravestone is a flat bronze marker furnished by the Army and detailing his name, final rank and years of service. We carefully followed Dad's wishes for his gravestone, including buying one big enough it wouldn't get buried should grass grow up around it someday.

It was very important to my father that he not disappear from this earth without a trace. "I did not want to just to have it all disappear down the drain when I died or something," he said. "I did not want that to be the end of it. I wanted to leave a little footprint there somewhere."

To twist a famous phrase from the late General Douglas MacArthur, old soldiers never die; they just write books.

— **William D. LaRue, 2015**

CHAPTER 1: Norwood

I was playing with my cousins in 1937, right around the Fourth of July, when I heard one yell, "Hey, Kenny, watch this!"

My cousins were busy lighting a bunch of firecrackers. They threw one down in the middle of the street and ran back. In seconds a loud explosion echoed through the neighborhood. They lit another and another. Sometimes, they'd put a can down with a firecracker under the edge. When it went off, the can shot about 15 feet in the air. Being I was only 5 years old, that was delightfully fun to watch.

I learned it was even okay if the firecracker didn't explode. If it was a dud, a cousin would pick it up, break it in two and stick a lit match to the powder inside. It made a sizzling sound and shot sparks.

I was excited when my cousins handed me a few. I got some matches and started lighting my firecrackers. *Bang! Bang! Bang!* I lit a fourth one, but this one was apparently a dud. I waited for what I thought was a long time before going over to break it in half. The second I picked it up, *Bang!* I looked down, and there was this huge gash in my right hand, gushing blood.

I started screaming and crying. My father came running from somewhere. I think he knew right away what happened. He picked me up, took me into the house, rinsed off the wound and wrapped my hand in a bandage.

He drove me downtown in our village of Norwood, New York, to see Dr. Henry Vinicor. Dr. Vinicor patched me up real good and gave me a tetanus shot. Then he looked at me sternly: "Don't play with any more firecrackers."

I never did. I had learned my lesson. Besides, after this injury and a similar one with another boy, the village banned private use of fireworks.

To this day, because of that firecracker, I carry a scar about an inch long on my right hand, just left of the index finger.

That's me on the left holding my brother Joe in Norwood sometime in the mid-1940s. Standing next to me is my sister, Jean; my father, Julius, my mother, Evelyn, and my brother Ronny.

Despite the occasional wounding, Norwood was a great place to grow up. Even the name conjures up mental pictures of an idyllic little community, something straight out of a Jimmy Stewart movie. It certainly seemed that way in the 1930s and 1940s, despite living lots of hard times during the Great

Depression and World War II.

Norwood is nestled in a valley along the Raquette River in the far reaches of northern New York. It's a few miles south of the Canadian border, kind of geographically and socially isolated from the rest of the country. We were so close to Canada we could smell smoke from forest fires every time they burned there in the summer. Norwood's population in 1940 was around 2,000. It was a mix of people of various ethnic groups, such as Irish, Italian, English and French, almost all white. I don't recall that there were any black families in the village at that time.

Chickens and Pigs and Fish, Oh, My!

I was born January 27, 1932, at the hospital down the road in Potsdam. I have a copy of the $54 bill for the 12-day hospital stay for Evelyn LaRue, including "11 days of daycare for baby."

I remember Mom as being young and pretty. She was so kind to my sister, Jean, and me, and later to my two much younger brothers, Ronny and Joe. We grew up thinking of her as almost a saint. My father, Julius, had a bad temper that was awfully scary when it was directed at you. Dad could peel the walls with his bad language, too. But he had a good heart in many ways and was very sentimental and protective of Mom and us kids. We didn't have a lot of money, but we never felt deprived growing up.

My father's first automobile, as I recall, was an Essex Sedan with wooden wheel spokes. It was difficult to start in the winter, so Dad put it up on blocks and drained it of antifreeze until spring. We didn't need a car most of the time. Back then,

Norwood had everything within walking distance – restaurants, churches, grocery stores, bank, schools and a movie theater. Sidewalks were often packed with shoppers.

There was a little candy store where my family also got soft drinks and other stuff. In those days, the display of penny candy was a veritable fantasy land for kids. We could have our choice from a whole case of different sweets, from Tootsie Rolls to suckers. There was even a candy stick with a ring on it for a penny. If I had a nickel, my day was made.

Like many others in Norwood at the time, we raised livestock right in our backyard next to the Victory Garden, which a lot of people grew during World War II. At one time we had about 200 chickens and a couple of pigs. After the pigs got big enough to be butchered, it was everything I could do to hang onto the rear end of the pig – back feet and everything – while Dad cut its throat. We got a lot of meat from those pigs. Dad made smoked hams out of them, some of the best I ever tasted.

Thanks to our chickens, we had so many fresh eggs we sold some to the neighbors. My job was to candle each one. I held them up to the light to make sure there wasn't a chick inside. There usually wasn't.

I also fed the chickens and gave them water every day before school. What a sight: I'd open up a door from the chicken coop and they would race down this long ramp, flying off the sides and making a big roar as they headed for the food and water. It was such a spectacle that some people came by just to watch.

My parents stand in their Victory Garden during World War II.

Mom let me know when it came time to kill a few chickens.

"I'm going to can today," she told me. "I want you to kill 10. Make sure you get good, fat ones."

She started to prepare the canning jars as I headed to the chicken yard. Typically, Ronny and Joe tagged along.

I looked for the first fat chicken that came my way. I grabbed it by the feet and tipped it upside down so it wouldn't peck at me. Nearby was a big block of wood. I laid the neck across it and – *whack!* – off with the head.

You know what they say about someone running around like a chicken with its head cut off? This is where that expression comes from: When I cut the head off, the chicken's body kept running for several seconds. It invariably would head right for Joe, sending him screaming and running for cover.

I kept killing chickens until I got the 10 that Mom wanted. First thing she did was soak each one in hot water so that the feathers would come off easier. My, those wet feathers stunk like the worst thing you can imagine. She laid these smelly, dead chickens out on newspaper on the kitchen table, and Jean and I had to start picking off the loose feathers. The chickens also had these pinfeathers – little dark things – and we had to get in there and pluck those out, too.

Mom canned a lot back then because we didn't have an electric refrigerator. All we had was an ice box, which was about as good as nothing. It would keep milk for a day or two. And the ice would melt out the top of that thing into a big pan on the bottom, and that pan would begin to run over. I'd notice that and pull it out. When I picked it up, it always spilled as I walked it to the sink.

Dad

During the Depression, Dad took almost any kind of job he could find to help put food on the table. For a while, he worked at Building 79 at the Alcoa plant in Massena. His boss was a really nasty guy, and my father could take only so much of it before he grabbed the boss and threatened to beat the shit out of him if he didn't leave him alone. Dad got fired over that.

My father went to work for the New York Central Railroad for quite a while. He rode on the freight trains that went back and forth through New York. His job was disconnecting cars and connecting them up again, and getting the trains in the right order. He often was gone for days at a time. Sometimes he had to stay overnight in Syracuse and come back on the train the next day.

He left the railroad in the 1940s for a job at the St. Regis Paper Co. mill a few miles away in Norfolk. He worked in the sulfite department for quite a long while. He even got me a job working there for three months in the summer of 1949.

I spent a lot of time with Dad while growing up. He took me fishing after I got to be about 10. We fished along on the shore of the Raquette River for a long time because we didn't have a boat. Dad started a smudge fire to get rid of the mosquitoes, and we'd fish from about a half-hour before dark until maybe an hour after dark. Fish would bite as fast as we could throw our lines in. The gaming laws at the time allowed each of us to have two lines. It was nothing to come home with a pail of 70 or 80 bullhead between the two of us. I would clean them and Mom cooked them up.

If we needed extra food, Dad didn't always follow the gaming rules. He sometimes brought along 10 empty beer bottles. He put plugs in the bottles, tied fishing line with bait to each one, and tossed them into the water. We'd pull out fish as fast as we could re-bait the hooks. Having 10 going at once was illegal, but we never got caught. During the war years, there weren't many game wardens around.

Dad taught me how to trap, muskrats mainly. We set the traps right along the river. He'd show me a muskrat hole, and he'd set the trap and drive a stake in it so it wouldn't get away. We skinned the muskrats and sold the pelts. We didn't do that too much, though, because it was a lot of work and the pelts weren't worth a lot.

Mom

After church on Sunday, Dad often would say, "Ma, why don't we go on a picnic today?" Of course, Mom had to do almost all the work to get the food ready. But he would help us load the car or go down and get gas so we had enough and we would head out.

The tires weren't so reliable back then, and during World War II you couldn't get new ones. Each tire had a tube inside, and it would regularly blow and we'd have to stop and patch it and re-inflate the tire. I saw times we'd have eight patches on a tube. On one family trip to Ogdensburg, we had three flats on the way and two on the way back. By the second or third patch, Dad was fuming so bad we dared not say a word.

Dad occasionally aimed his explosive temper at Mom, but he always immediately regretted it. He would turn around and be awfully nice to her and tell her how much he loved her.

"You don't know how lucky you are to have such a wonderful mother," he would say over and over to us kids. Of course, it was easy to believe him because, indeed, she was a great mom.

My mother was born in Canada to Protestant parents. Dad was Catholic, and so she converted. I never thought too much about her faith until one time when I was a young teenager and went upstairs while she was there. She didn't hear me coming. There she was on her knees next to the bed, praying. That really impressed me because Mom read a lot and was so intelligent and very much with it. From that day forward, I truly believed in God and believed in my religion.

Dad liked a good drink. But he didn't get drunk very often because my mother didn't like it, even though he was always the happiest drunk you ever saw. He'd get red and shiny, and he would laugh at everything. There was nothing my mother would say that wouldn't make him laugh.

One day she went by him at the kitchen table and he goosed her in the behind. She happened to have a boiler cover in her hand. And because his pinch startled her, she out of reflex hit him in the shins hard enough to almost break his leg. All he did was sit there and laugh and laugh and laugh. It must have hurt like hell. But he still laughed.

Another thing he did was to take off a cardboard cap on a milk bottle back when the cream rose to the top. There would be a little bit of cream stuck to the cap. He's go over and touch Mom on the face with that and say, "There, I'll give you a peaches and cream complexion." Boy, she hated that.

One time he sprayed a little water on her. Next thing I knew she had a glass of water, and he was racing out the door as fast as he could. When they got outside, she threw the water in hopes of getting him. The neighbors must have thought we were nuts.

Mom's parents, James and Emily Emburey, moved to Norwood with my mother and her brothers in the mid-1920s. Grandpa Emburey had served with the Canadian Expeditionary Force during World War I after enlisting at age 33 in 1916. He fought as a machine gunner in several battles in France. My father loved to go over to visit my grandfather and hear his stories about being in the war. Along the way he met my mother and they soon fell in love.

I heard a lot about the military while growing up. My mother's older brother, Cecile, signed up for the U.S. Army in 1927 and served two enlistments. He died tragically at age 29 in 1941 from severe burns. He was a passenger in a tractor-trailer that burst into flames after it flipped near Middletown, New York, while hauling sugar.

Then there was my great-grandfather Julius LaRue (my father was named after him), who fought for the Union Army in the Civil War. He enlisted at age 27 in 1863. Records show he spent much of his later years unsuccessfully applying for military payments for an injury to his side when he was whacked by a plank while in the Army.

Jean

As close as I was to Mom, she spent more time with my sister, Jean, who was just two years younger than me. Being she was the girl of the family, in those days Jean had to learn how to sew, clean and cook. Mom also taught her strong moral values. Jean was always a very nice girl, and in school she was very respected by the other kids because of that. At the same time, Jean didn't take any malarkey. If you talked nasty to her, she let you know in a hell of a hurry to knock it off.

Jean and I loved to play Ante Over. We'd stand on each side of the house to play the game. One of us would toss the ball over the roof to the other, who had to catch it without the ball hitting the ground. When Mom and Dad headed to the movies, I'd always be after Jean to play the game, even though they always warned us not to do it because it could damage the roof.

"Mom and Dad don't really want us to do this," Jean would say. But the minute I threw the ball over the roof, she was right there playing the game.

As a young kid, I was probably your typical brat. When my cousin and best friend Bob Christian came over to the house, we used to play cowboys and Indians. I always wanted him to be the bad guy and me the good guy so I could shoot him. Or, if it was us playing Gene Autry and the villain, he'd play the villain. We'd go around slapping our hips and pretending to ride our horses around the house.

Ronny and Joe

I never really played with my two brothers. There was an eight-year difference in age between Ronny and me, and 11 years for Joe. When I was a teenager, they were just in the road most of the time.

Ronny was a pretty quiet kid, but Joe was a real devil then. He was very mischievous, except when my father was around.

One time my mother told Joe to do something and he said, "No."

Joe forgot that our father was in the living room. Dad let out a bellow. "What did you say?"

Joe replied, "I said I was going to do that right away," and he proceeded to do it right away.

World War II

In 1940, as the winds of war were approaching, troops moved into northern New York to conduct maneuvers, some held right in the Norwood area. Suddenly, there were soldiers everywhere. Empty cartridges and regimental crests became collector's items. At times there were howitzers in the streets, and blimps and bi-wing planes in the air.

That's me at far left playing soldier during World War II with friends in Norwood.

It was a warm and muggy Saturday on August 17, 1940, when my mother brought my sister and me to Main Street to watch as President Franklin Roosevelt rode by in an open touring car with New York Gov. Herbert Lehman while visiting the military maneuvers. It wasn't until years later that I comprehended how lucky we were to see the president in person.

On Sunday, December 7, 1941, our family traveled to Ogdensburg to visit my father's sister. When the kids, who were outside playing, ran into the house, the grownups ordered us all to be quiet. They were glued to the radio. The Japanese had attacked the U.S. base in Pearl Harbor. The adults all knew this meant we would soon be at war.

On the way home, I sat quietly as my parents discussed the probability of food rationing, and they agreed we better stock up on the things that would be scarce. They were right. During the war years, almost everything was rationed. I could only get new shoes when our ration stamp came around. For a while, I went to school with a piece of cardboard tucked inside my shoe to cover a big hole on the bottom. When I stepped into a puddle, it would all but melt that cardboard. First thing I knew the bottom of my foot would be touching the ground again.

The war years also brought mandatory blackouts to Norwood, just in case the enemy thought about bombing our village. Air raid wardens (usually guys too old for the service) patrolled the streets at night. They knocked at your door and ordered you to turn off your lights if you didn't have your shades pulled tightly closed. Many nights, my sister and I knelt in the window in that darkness and watched for falling stars for what seemed like hours.

At school, teachers had savings bond sales to raise money for the war effort. We'd bring in money to buy savings stamps. When a book of them was filled, it could be redeemed for an $18.75 bond, which matured years later at $25.

From time to time, the teachers would ask classmates how their older brothers were doing in the service. Some had been wounded or captured in battle. Others never came home. Windows in certain houses around town began to display stars on them. A blue star meant a son was in the service. A gold star meant he had been killed.

As children, we never had any doubt America would win the war, thanks partly to all that propaganda going on at the time. At the theater, movies stirred hatred for the Germans and Japanese. We just thought that we were tougher than them and that good wins out over evil. We did not realize until later how iffy the war was going from time to time, and how we could have lost it rather easily.

I remember we were up at our Adirondacks camp on Sterling Pond in 1945 when we heard on the radio that the Americans had dropped the atomic bomb on Hiroshima, Japan. We didn't know much about the bomb back then, but Dad accurately guessed the war wasn't going to last much longer.

The first thing Dad did after the war was to buy four brand new tires and put them on the car, with all new tubes.

The Car Accident

In fall 1945, my father was driving to the paper mill in Norfolk one morning when he pulled over his Model A Ford to pick up another worker. Dad was just ready to pull away when a vehicle crashed into the back of his car. The truck box Dad built into the back drove him against the steering wheel, severely injuring his back and stomach.

The other driver, who was just 29, sped away. Police caught him about an hour later hiding in an old ice house in Norfolk. He had some bruises on his nose and cheek. It turns out that he earlier hit a car in Potsdam and fled that crash, too.

The man pleaded guilty to leaving the scene of an accident in Potsdam and was fined $10, according to the Potsdam Herald-Recorder. In Norfolk, he was fined $55 for leaving the scene of an accident, driving with a revoked license and driving an unregistered motor vehicle.

Dad was in the hospital for about four months. I don't know all of his injuries, but he had blood clots that doctors were afraid might go to his heart. At one point the doctors told my mother they weren't sure Dad was going to live.

I came home one day and saw my mother sitting in the living room in a rocking chair, crying.

"They said your dad's awful bad," she told me.

"Is he going to be okay?"

She shook her head. "I don't know."

Fortunately, Dad got better, although slowly. We had a bed set up in the living room. A few days after he came home from the hospital, he had a sharp pain; apparently, a blood clot went right through his heart. Because he was only 35, he was strong enough to survive it. We called an ambulance and they took him right back to the hospital for another week or so before they sent him home again.

He was out of work for a long time, and we had big medical bills to pay. The other driver didn't have car insurance. We had to sell our camp on Sterling Pond and a small farm just to pay the bills.

In 1947, a judge granted my father $16,650 in a judgment of uncontested negligence against the other driver. That was a fantastic amount of money back then. But the man disappeared. Dad never saw a penny of it.

My Bland Ambitions

I knew in high school there was almost no chance I could afford to go to college. Back then the only ones in my village who went to college were those whose parents had a lot of money or who went in the military and got G.I. Bill benefits.

I'm standing in the top row, center, in a yearbook photo during my senior year at Norwood High School.

I felt no great need to join the Army so I could go to college.

There were plenty of good jobs that paid pretty well for those with just a high school education. Alcoa in Massena was a great place to work; they employed a couple of thousand in those days. There were also two thriving paper mills – one in Norfolk and one in Unionville, a little hamlet near Norwood. The railroad was running big-time and you could get a job with them.

You might not be rich, but you did pretty well for yourself without going to college. And you could have a family and, on that one salary, could support everybody. You didn't have to have your wife working out, because it wasn't necessary in those days.

From first grade until sixth grade, I was about the top student in my Norwood class almost every year. Either top or two or three. Always. But as I went into seventh and eighth grades, something changed. I tended to be a little bit lazy. I didn't want the good grades so much. I wanted to do the things that interested me. I loved industrial arts – which everyone called "shop." I took that as my minor and accounting as my major when I got into high school. I enjoyed tremendously working with power tools and lathes, and learning how to do electrical wiring and other practical things like that.

Still, I didn't have bad grades, maybe an 85 average or so. The only class I came close to failing was typing. Typing was the first thing where I had to be ambidextrous rather than mental. I got a 65 with a circle around it, which meant I passed. Barely.

I didn't play sports in high school. I might have been able to make a team if I put a lot of effort into it. But my father wanted me home. He always had work for me to do. If I had joined a team, at first, "Well, great, my son is going to play sports." But the first night I wasn't home when he wanted me to fix something, he would have started to complain and bitch, and first thing you know I would have had to quit, because I wasn't getting the work done at home. When he wanted you there, you better damn well be there. It didn't matter what it was. No excuses. And I knew that. I just didn't go out for sports for that reason. I would hurry up and do all my homework in my study halls so I didn't have any at night at home. (My senior year when I was 18, I went out for the school play and had a lead role. I guess by then I figured Dad couldn't say too much anymore.)

I'm sure some of my lack of interest in school came from discovering the opposite sex. I had my first crush in 11th grade when Helen Weaver moved from Massena to Norwood. She was very pretty and very flirtatious. Before long, we were going to basketball games and doing homework together. But we didn't really date. One day, I learned she was going out with one of my best friends. He was a great guy and I didn't resent him for it. But it devastated me.

I was 17 when I first met Carol LaPlante at Joe's Restaurant in Norfolk, not far from where she lived. She was blonde and very nice-looking, so I noticed her there right away. I didn't know at the time she was only 14. She just looked so much older. I saw her again that summer at The Coach bar in Norfolk, and I danced with her most of the evening. I also saw her at some of the high school dances. Even though she had a boyfriend at the time, she always found time to break away to dance with me.

My senior year I started going out with a girl from Norwood who was also very pretty and very nice, too. But then I started going to Massena. The girls there were very aggressive. If they wanted to go out with you, they let you know.

Well, I had to unload this girl in Norwood before I could go out with any girls in Massena. But I was too much of a coward to do so in person. I sent her a letter. I told her how much I thought of her, but I didn't want to go out with anybody, and all that business. Of course, she showed it to all her friends. She was very hurt by it. I really felt bad in a way, but I really wanted to break up.

My senior year, I must have gone out with six or seven different girls in Massena. One was Sally Christy, who worked at the soda fountain at Newberry's in the city. She was about a year older than me but so cute you couldn't help but notice her. She was tiny, and always pushing her glasses up on her nose. We started dating steady, and she became by girlfriend in my senior year.

As graduation approached in June 1950, I was pretty excited about what lay ahead. I planned to find a good job and spend more time with Sally. I even thought she might be one I would marry. Little did I know that the sirens of war would soon cast a sour note at what was to have been one of the happiest days of our young lives.

CHAPTER 2: Private LaRue

My high school graduation speaker dramatically tore up his notes as he stood before us in the Music Hall in Norwood. It was June 27, 1950. That same day, President Harry Truman announced he was sending U.S. troops to war to stop the North Korean invasion of South Korea that began two days earlier.

"I had written these up to speak to you tonight. These aren't relevant anymore," the Rev. Dr. John R. Williams told our class. "There's a war on. Most of you young guys are going to be in the service in a very short period of time."

His topic was "What to Do with Your Life." He talked about the G.I. Bill and all the opportunities for education in the service, and how there we might find what it was we wanted to do with our lives.

I stand with Mom and Dad in my high school graduation cap and gown in June 1950.

I wasn't convinced, at least not right away. I needed time to consider what I was getting into. Joining the military was a pretty big step.

The Korean War seemed to come out of nowhere. Located on a peninsula just west of Japan, Korea had been under brutal Japanese rule before it was torn into North and South at the end of World War II. The Russian Communists grabbed the North above the 38th Parallel, while the South remained a free country under the protection of the United States.

After North Korea invaded, the United Nations voted for armed intervention by U.N. forces to the defense of South Korea. The U.S. Army and forces by other nations would have boots on the ground in no time.

About eight guys in my class enlisted in the first three weeks after war broke out, and I began to think it was time for me to do the same. If all my classmates enlisted, I didn't want to be the only one not to go. I knew they would probably be drafting anyway, and in fact the U.S. did start the draft in a few months.

Growing up, I had a certain idealized version of the military, but I also knew from listening to all the guys coming home from World War II that the Army was a tough place and that sergeants could be very miserable. The Army is almost an absolute dictatorship sometimes. I knew basic training was going to be so humiliating to an individual – because they needed to break your spirit to the point where you obey instantly any command. I didn't look forward to that.

Around mid-July 1950, I was downtown when a guy I knew from school stopped me. His name was Paul. He was a grade behind me but the same age, so I knew him pretty well. He got right to the question of the day.

"So, Kenny, are you going to enlist in the Army?"

"Oh, I'm thinking about it. I haven't made up my mind yet," I said, eying the smoke from my Camel cigarette.

Paul hiked his body up a bit straighter and looked me in the eye.

"Well, I'm going over tomorrow to Ogdensburg and enlist. Why don't you come over with me?"

I shrugged. "I'm still thinking about it."

"Well, you big chicken shit," Paul said. "C'mon go with me and we'll enlist together."

I thought about it a little more. I didn't like being called chicken shit. I did like the idea of not going alone to enlist.

"OK, what time do you want to meet in the morning?" I asked.

He grinned. "That's swell. Come over to my house at 8 o'clock and we'll go."

That evening, I told my mother and father I was signing up for the Army. They weren't thrilled about it, but they understood because it seemed the rest of the men my age were signing up.

The next morning, I knocked on the door at Paul's house right at 8 o'clock. His mother answered.

"I'm looking for Paul," I said.

"He's still in bed, asleep."

I explained how he had asked me to come over so we could go together to enlist in the Army. It was the first she heard about it.

"You go in and pound on his door and wake him up and ask him what the hang is going on," she told me.

I rapped several times. The door finally opened, but his eyes were almost shut.

"Oh, geez," he whined. "I don't think I'm going to go after all."

What? "You talked me into this yesterday," I said, "and I went home and told my parents and everybody I was going into the service, and now you're telling me I have to go by myself?"

"Well," he said with a sigh, "I've been thinking about it and I decided I'm not going to go after all."

I was furious, but all I said was, "Okay," and left.

At that point, I felt I was committed to the Army. I would look like a fool or worse if I backed out now after telling people I was going in. Plus, I convinced myself at that point it was the right thing to do. So, without going back home, I hitchhiked on my own the 30 miles to Ogdensburg. I signed papers at the enlistment center, and the sergeant gave me the date to report.

The day after I enlisted, Myron "Punchy" Palmer came over to talk. Everybody called him Punchy because he had taken up amateur boxing. He was a couple of grades behind me in school, but he was old enough to go in the service.

"Hey, Ken. Somebody told me you enlisted," he said.

"Yeah."

"Boy, I wish I had known. I would have liked to go with you."

In a few days I said goodbye to my family. I didn't know it then, but I would never see my Grandpa Emburey again. He died four months later, and by then I was unable to get leave to attend the funeral.

You're In the Army Now

On Saturday, July 15, the Army herded me and other enlistees from towns and villages all around northern New York onto a Greyhound bus out of Ogdensburg, and we headed 130 miles south to Syracuse. Among those on the bus was Punchy Palmer and another Norwood guy, George Harris, who graduated high school in 1949.

The Army put us up in Syracuse's historic Yates Hotel, which has since been torn down. The first time I ever saw television was in the hotel bar. It was a wrestling match.

I sent a postcard home right away:

> Dear Mom, Dad and kids,
>
> Got to Syracuse this morning. Having good time. Don't worry, I'll write later. We have a beautiful hotel room and swell meals. Ken

The Army told us to report a few blocks away at the Chimes Building on South Salina Street, where doctors gave us physicals and we took a bunch of tests to prove how much smarts we had.

After four days, just one guy in our group was rejected. He had to go back home because his glasses were about an inch thick. He was very disappointed.

The (Syracuse) Post-Standard published a large picture the next day showing 27 of us recruits posing with Major H.S. Oram giving us "final instructions," according to the caption. Several of the recruits show big smiles, but I look pretty grim.

The Army swore us in right there, then took us by train on the New York Central to New York City. We switched over at Penn Station to another train, which took us to a New Jersey bus stop. A bus brought us right into Fort Dix, the East Coast troop-training center, about 30 miles from Philadelphia.

When our bus pulled up, that's when the yelling began. We hadn't even gotten off the vehicle when sergeants began shouting at us to hurry up and get moving and a lot of other things. I knew there was going to be lots of yelling, but we still looked at each other as if to say: Did we just make a big mistake?

It was late at night when they took us into this barracks, an old, wooden structure straight out of World War I, all very spartan. We had to crowd around while this sergeant showed us how to make a bunk, and he bounced a quarter off it to show how tight the bedding had to be. Then each one of us had to make our bunk, and he came around and checked them. Mine was satisfactory. Then he told us to get ready and go to bed.

It didn't seem like any time before we had to get up. I think it was 5 a.m. I wasn't used to getting up that early.

Our first trip to the mess hall was very discouraging. The eggs were floating in grease, and the rest of our breakfast was not very appetizing, but I ate it. I was that hungry.

The Army was in a hurry for fresh bodies in Korea, I guess. The orientation manual they gave us at Fort Dix outlined a 14-week program. However, the other recruits and I were squeezed into an eight-week program. The good news is that we got out of basic in almost half the normal time. The bad news is that the intensity was turned up to make sure we learned the essentials.

They handed us a list of our scheduled activities during the first four days:

ARRIVAL DAY - Bath and Haircut

1st Day
0730 Reception Orientation
0830 Medical Processing (Physical Inspection, Profile, Medical Inspection)
0900 Clothing Issue
1300 Articles of War Read and Explained; Film (Passaic Lounge)
1500 Required Talks and Films
1900 Supervised Marking of Clothing and Equipment

2nd Day
0800 Testing I

1330 Testing II

3rd Day
0730 Inoculation, X-Ray, Serology, Vaccination and Blood Type
0830 Physical Aptitude Test for MVO
1230 Insurance, Bonds and Allotments
1530 Troop Information Program (I & E Classroom)
*1630 Partial Pay
*Paid on the afternoon of the third day if possible; if not, on the afternoon of the fourth day of processing

4th Day
0730 Classification and Assignment Interview and Chaplain's Interview (Concurrently - Building T-19

"DO NOT GO ABSENT WITHOUT LEAVE," the schedule warned. It was signed W.D. McDonnell, Major, Infantry, Commanding.

I didn't get new clothing right away. To make us look uniform, each of us was given a rubber raincoat to wear over our civilian clothes. We were not allowed to unbutton them, despite the July heat, and we sweated like pigs as we ran from place to place.

The first week we were segregated from the rest of the Fort Dix troops while we were tested, taught the rules, fitted for uniforms and had the closest haircut of our lives. All the time we were being shouted at for not moving fast enough or doing what we were told.

A Clean Rifle

The beginning of the second week, we were moved to a basic training company that we would be with for the remainder of our stay. If we thought we were going through hell before, this was hell with the heat turned up. Exercise consisted of every movement ever invented, done over and over.

We had to learn how to march in formation and how to take apart a rifle into pieces, clean them, and put them all back together. The first time I did it, the sergeant came by to inspect. He ran his fingers up and down the barrel and peered inside.

"Not clean enough." He threw it back at me.

I did it again. It didn't take long to learn to clean things thoroughly, that doing so was as important as doing it in a hurry.

Our life would not have been complete without KP (kitchen police) duty. I washed dishes. I peeled enough potatoes until I swore I had enough for every soldier in the Army.

But I adjusted. I even adjusted to the yelling. I knew from what I'd read or seen in the movies that they would be yelling at you and trying to break your spirit, and they did.

One of the older recruits who had previously served in the military offered me a piece of advice: "Just do whatever they tell you to do. Don't fight it, and you'll get along."

I kept that advice in my head, and if I was given an order, I said, "Yes, sir" or "No, sir." And, hell, I didn't have any problem. Oh, they still yelled at me. But they wouldn't pursue it any further because I had already learned what they wanted me to do.

That was true except for one corporal who bordered on sadistic. He seemed to delight at finding fault where there was none, yelling when there was no reason. The guys called him The Rat. He even looked like a rat, with prominent teeth in the front.

The Perks of Being a Platoon Guide

I was out in the field one day having a smoking break when a sergeant came over to me. "The captain wants to see you right away," he said.

I put my cigarette out and went over to where the captain was visiting nearby. He started asking me questions about where I was from and what I did in high school. The sergeant stood right there behind me as this is going on, and he kept prodding me to say "sir" more often in my answers.

"I don't want to hear any sentence out of you that doesn't have 'sir' in it," the sergeant barked.

I was trying to talk to the captain, while listening to what the sergeant was telling me to do, and I kept wondering what was going on.

What it turned out: The captain was thinking of making me one of the platoon guides because my test marks came back strong. I was told I had the highest of anybody in my company.

My official Army photo taken at Fort Dix around September 1950. The Army ordered each of us to have our pictures taken, but they still made us pay for them.

Indeed, I became one of the platoon guides, which are the top persons among the recruits. That meant I was at the head of a marching group. The others had to follow me. Of course, I wasn't that adept at marching, but I managed to really concentrate because I didn't want to screw up and lose the position.

Once I got to be a platoon guide, my sergeant in the barracks treated me totally different. He treated me as the leader of the group.

One day, he said, "I want this barracks cleaned from stem to stern, and LaRue you're in charge."

I began to help with this cleaning. I didn't want to stand there and let everybody else do the work. But the sergeant stopped me and said, "LaRue, you're supervising. You don't clean."

After he left, I was standing there when The Rat came in and looked at me.

"LaRue, how come you're not working with the rest of these guys?"

I said, "I'm supposed to be in charge."

He thought that was bullshit, and said so. "That's no excuse. You get in there with a rag and you start cleaning with the rest of the guys." Then the corporal went into another room, and I started cleaning again.

The sergeant came back and said, "LaRue, I said that you're just supposed to be supervising the other guys."

I said, "The corporal has just told me I was to do the cleaning, too."

Now the sergeant was spitting mad. He went plowing down the hall into the other room and I could hear some yelling, and the next thing I knew he was back and said, "LaRue, you do what I told you, not what he told you."

When I had no assigned duties, one place I found that was a sanctuary for me was the church at Fort Dix. I went there a lot because I could kneel and pray and think and not have anybody on my tail all the time.

In case I needed any other religious reinforcement, shortly after I arrived for basic training, my parents received this very nice letter from the Catholic chaplain at Fort Dix:

Dear Catholic Parents,

I am Father Lynch, the Catholic Priest who will serve your son while he is at Fort Dix.

He is now in the Army! Well do I know how much you miss him from your home and miss your daily contact with him. We can and do help him – yes, we, YOU and I, his parents and his Catholic priest by our continual interest, encouragement and prayers, can be of immense assistance to him in his Army life.

What shall you do? 1. Write him encouraging and cheerful letters. 2. Remind him to be faithful in his morning and evening prayers. 3. Tell him to attend Mass every Sunday and to receive Holy Communion twice a month. 4. Encourage him to lead a good life by observing the Commandments of God and of our Catholic church. If these suggestions are followed, your son will be pleasing in the sight of God and shall bring untold joy to you and the family.

Would you receive Holy Communion on Sunday for your son? Will you recite your rosary for him? May I be personal? As long as I have been in the Army I know that every month my mother receives Holy Communion for me and that she never closes her eyes in sleep before she has recited her rosary to ask Mary's protection upon her Priest-soldier-son. I ask and urge you to do the same for your soldier-son. You will do that, won't you? In every letter, remind your son about Holy Communion.

I shall do all I can for your son while he is at Fort Dix.

Write to him and tell him you will go to Holy Communion and recite your rosary for him. Feel free to write to me at any time. I am at your service.

May God bless and protect you.

Father Robert E. Lynch

P.S. The Pope has granted the men and women in the Armed Forces the special privilege of attending Mass in the evening. Ask your son to come a few times each week.

Another sanctuary for me was the USO in Philadelphia. Most recruits got a pass every two or three weeks. Because I was a platoon guide, I got one every weekend.

When a group in our company decided to travel together one weekend, we had a choice to see Philadelphia or to watch the Dodgers play ball at Ebbets Field in Brooklyn. I was tom between the two, but I decided to go to Philly to see Independence Hall, the Liberty Bell, Betsy Ross' home, the Aquarium and the Museum of Art.

It was raining and gloomy in the city when I first visited, and the dark, old streets seemed magical – not much different from what they might have been in Benjamin Franklin's time. To stand where our forefathers signed the Declaration of independence and to touch the Liberty Bell was the culmination of all my history lessons.

They had a USO service club there on 57th Street in Philadelphia. It was like $1 to stay overnight. They had dances there every weekend. I continued to visit Philadelphia and its

USO every weekend until I shipped out of Fort Dix.

Most letters I wrote home I addressed to Mom, but this postcard I mailed to my father:

> September 4, 1950
>
> Dear Dad,
>
> Philly is a nice town. You should see all the women. Blondes, too. I'm on a three-day pass.
>
> Love,
>
> Ken

During most of my eight weeks at Fort Dix, the war was going badly for the United Nations forces under American command. But then in the fall, U.S. Gen. Douglas MacArthur came through with a stroke of genius. He had troops invade at Inchon, half-way up the Korean peninsula. He drove right across and cut quite a lot of the enemy off. Of course, without having a source of supplies from the north, the enemy quickly knew they were going to run out of ammo and they were all going to be dead if they stayed there. So, they ran like hell as fast as they could north. A lot of them got killed trying to get there. We had the planes and tanks and everything, and we wiped them out where we could.

Once he got started, MacArthur drove right toward the North Korean border with China. U.N. forces had almost complete control of both North and South Korea in a short period of time. There was even talk the war would be over by Christmas.

Goodbye to The Rat

There were three possibilities for recruits once they finished basic training at Fort Dix. They could remain there with one of the units. They could be sent to school to learn a specialty. Or, they could be sent to an Army division, possibly one in combat.

They asked me what I was interested in doing. I told them I'd like to learn radio repair, thinking it might also make for a good career after I got out of the service. Instead, I got orders to go directly to Fort Bliss, Texas, to attend radar repair school.

I also was promoted from recruit (E-1) to private (E-2) with a bump in salary. But because I wasn't sent to radar school by an Army division, I would have no unit to promote me further until I left radar school.

My last memory of Fort Dix was an odd but pleasing one. As we were boarding a truck for the train station, I looked over and saw The Rat weeding a flower bed. Apparently, the gossip was true: He had been demoted and given garden duty for urinating on a captain's desk.

Several of us new privates thought about yelling out, "Hey, Rat." But by then we were so afraid of him, we didn't want to take the chance this was an Army trick to test our discipline, so we all kept our mouths shut.

Four of us from Fort Dix – three white soldiers and one black – were sent together to radar school without a furlough, even though we had time off coming. On the way we became good friends as we traveled three or four days by civilian passenger train, sleeping in very comfortable roomettes. In St. Louis, we transferred to a second train that took us through Oklahoma into Texas and all the way across to the southwestern corner of the state. Our destination was the city of El Paso, just outside Fort Bliss and right on the border of Mexico. Fort Bliss was just 100 miles from the White Sands Missile Base and about 140 miles from Carlsbad Caverns.

Southern Cooking

When we arrived in El Paso, we were very hungry for something more than dining car fare and decided to have lunch at the restaurant in the train station. We just sat down together at the lunch counter when a waitress came over.

"I can wait on you and you and you," she said, pointing to me and the two other white guys, then looked over at our black friend. "But not you. You have to go back there."

She pointed to a segregated spot in the back of the restaurant. Being young Northern boys, we decided to show how we wouldn't tolerate racism. We explained that we were all soldiers going to Fort Bliss and that we wanted to sit together.

"Either he sits in the back or y'all leave," she said quietly.

We got huffy and decided we weren't going to put up with this. We got up and left the restaurant. Of course, then we had to figure out where to eat, and we soon realized that no place around would serve the four of us together.

Our black friend spoke up then. "Look, I don't want any trouble. I'll go find a place by myself."

By then we were too hungry to disagree. After he left, we went back inside and ordered lunch.

Because we didn't have to report to Fort Bliss until the next day, the three of us got a cheap hotel room, left our belongings and went out on the town. We returned to the room sometime around midnight and immediately fell asleep, exhausted, in our three small beds.

When I awoke in the morning, one of the guys, who was from Rochester, New York, was standing on a dresser looking through a transom into the next room.

He had a big smile as he quietly motioned us to join him.

"Come on. Come on," he whispered.

I jumped up on the dresser and peered into the next room, where a couple were too busy having sex to notice they were being spied upon.

All of a sudden, the guy from Rochester started to fall. He instinctively grabbed the curtain on the transom to catch himself, and he tore it off as he loudly clattered to the floor. We all started giggling.

Suddenly, in the next room we could hear conversation. Its door soon opened, and we heard a man's footsteps heading quickly down the hall.

A few seconds later, we heard the same door open again, then a knock on our door. We stayed very still. Was the woman angry? Was she a prostitute? Our young minds raced with the possibilities. After a while, we heard her go back to her room, lock the door and leave. For about 10 minutes, we just sat there fearing she might be lurking outside our door.

One of us finally peeked out. There was nobody in sight. We had all our stuff with us and ready to go, so we hiked out of there and down the stairs and out into the street. We caught a bus and went into Fort Bliss.

The guy checking us in at the Army post wanted to know how come we arrived the day before but didn't show up until then.

"This is the date we were supposed to appear. We thought we had a little time to ourselves," I said. He didn't argue the point. He just processed us and assigned us to barracks.

But It Was a Dry Heat

Fort Bliss was built on the desert, just outside El Paso. In mid-September 1950, the base consisted mostly of Quonset huts, except for the school buildings, which were two stories high with tan stucco in a Spanish style with red tile roofs. Fort Bliss was mainly an artillery training base, with a radar and guided missiles school. Several World War II German missiles decorated the area of the school.

The first three months of radar school consisted of classroom training in mathematics and algebra and the principles of radar. The rest of the eleven months involved on-the-job training on SCR 584 radars. They were located in huge trailers filled with electronics that were very modern for their time. The radar connected up to the artillery pieces. If everything was properly adjusted, the radar would lock onto a practice drone and the artillery would fire at it, knocking it down. In actual use, soldiers were more likely to hit the towing plane than the drone. It took a lot of experience to fine-tune the whole thing so it worked properly.

Among my radar-school classmates was George Harris from Norwood, who also transferred here from Fort Dix. We hung out quite a bit together. I also made good friends with several of the other soldiers in radar school, and I collected a lot of goofy photos of us posing with each other.

I pretend to break up a fight at Fort Bliss with radar school classmates George Harris, left, and Dewey Yeagar. It must have been a Sunday morning because I'm dressed in my church clothes.

Fort Bliss treated us to a nice feast on Christmas, my first December 25 ever celebrated away from Norwood. Our meal included roast turkey, cranberries, gravy, dressing, whipped potatoes, sweet potatoes, french green beans, rolls, salad, pie and coffee.

I was so impressed that, shortly afterward, I included a copy of the menu with this letter home.

Dear Mom,

Here is our Christmas Dinner Menu.

I went to Midnight Mass with George (Harris) at St. Michael's Cathedral last night.

Thanks for all the Christmas presents. The cookies and fudge was swell and sure helps keep up my morale.

Tell Dad thanks a lot for the lighter. There was nothing in the world I needed worse. Thank Jean for the lovely leather case and toilet articles. It is really swell. Thank Ronny and Joe for the stationery. That is really a help. Envelopes are sometimes hard to get.

But my best Christmas present was the telephone call (Dec. 24). It was the best present I could get except being home. I received your letter the day before saying you would call.

About 7 o'clock in the morning the CQ came and woke me. He told me I had a long distance call and to ring Operator 5 in Potsdam. I called and in five minutes the call was through to you. It was awfully nice hearing your voices once more.

Will close now. I will write again soon. Hope
you all had a Merry Christmas.

Love, Ken

I passed the radar school's required 64-question written exam
on basic electronics on January 24, 1951, three days short of
my 19th birthday.

About half of the way through our training, we were taken out
into the desert to a bombing range, where we stood on a hill,
while below us planes bombed, fired bullets and dropped
napalm. It was a very exciting day for all of us.

Life at Fort Bliss fell into a routine very quickly. The weather
was almost always hot, but it was a dry heat and didn't seem
all that uncomfortable.

Blowing sand was probably the only hardship we faced. While
I was there, one sandstorm got so bad that visibility was
almost zero. To cross the parade field to the mess hall, I had
to hang onto the chain-link fence to find the way. People who
had cars at the base complained afterward that the sand took
the paint off their vehicles. The sand accumulated on the
inside sills of the windows and even on our bunks. After the
sandstorm, we had to remove everything from the barracks,
shake out our bedding, sweep all the sand out and put
everything back again.

On April 18, 1951, I was in the bathroom in the barracks at
about 11:30 a.m. when I heard a loud crash in the parade
field. A four-engine B-50 bomber out of Biggs Air Force Base

had crash-landed. The pilot had managed to avoid a school full of kindergarteners, but the plane hit an empty school bus, plowed through some fences and then burst into flames. I quickly got out of the barracks and ran to the field, which was already filled with hundreds of guys.

The crew of the plane jumped out onto the ground as we watched, except for one unlucky soul, the radar operator, who died inside. Flames from the plane burned it completely, along with a fire truck that had pulled up next to it. We noticed that part of a wing was embedded in the bus.

Suddenly, there were MPs all over the place taking cameras away from everyone, stripping out the film and handing back the photographic gear. The crash for some reason had a veil of Cold War secrecy. The next day, the newspaper reported that the military refused to disclose the plane's destination or its mission. But the gossip among soldiers was that there might have been nuclear weapons aboard.

In Korea, U.N. forces had not obtained that predicted quick end to the war. General MacArthur had succeeded in driving the North Koreans right through to the Chinese border. But, all of a sudden, the Chinese decided, "Hey, we don't want them taking over part of our Communist empire." So they came in with about 2 million Chinese in a very surprise move. Suddenly, U.N. troops faced hordes of Chinese coming the other way. To survive, our troops had to run south like hell to get away. And a lot of them couldn't get away fast enough. But fortunately many traveled east to Hamhung Harbor and loaded on ship after ship and got out of there.

Soon, the U.N. forces regrouped and returned south below the Chinese and stopped them, and our people started driving the enemy north like they did the North Koreans previously. (This is the reason some have called this the "Yo-yo War.")

As battles raged, I got word around June 1951 that my one of my Norwood classmates, Bobby Cutler, was missing in action in Korea. He had been caught in some ferocious combat while serving with the Army's 38th Infantry Regiment, 2nd Infantry Division. As bad as I felt for Bobby and his family, I was relieved to be in radar school studying a skill that I hoped would keep me out of combat.

My classroom work was interesting, I enjoyed repairing radars, and there was always time off to relax and enjoy myself. In February, a group of us attended a Harlem Globetrotters game in El Paso. It was their first team, too, and a ticket only cost $1.50.

The Truth About Alligators

The alligator pool was a favorite spot in El Paso, seen here in 1951.

One of my favorite spots in downtown El Paso was San Jacinto Plaza, which had a pool with several big alligators in it. It was right next to the Hotel Paso del Norte and across the road from the Hilton Hotel. The pool had a little stone fence around it, high enough the alligators couldn't get out. We used to go down there and watch the alligators. They wouldn't move for hours. We would yell and make all kinds of motions to get the alligators to move. If you stood there long enough, or poked one with a stick or something, finally – *bang!* – it would snap at you.

One day I was downtown when I spotted this really good-looking blonde selling magazines on the street corner. She came up to me, very flirty.

"Sir," she said with a big smile, "would you like to buy a subscription to a very good magazine at a great discount?"

Her name was Bobbie. I had no interest in the magazines that she or her bunch of compadres were selling. I figured it was just a con anyway. But, just because Bobbie was so good-looking, I spent as much time as I could listening to her give her best pitch. I eventually parted with $2 for a two-year subscription to Florida Speaks Sportsman magazine. It was worth two bucks just to talk to her.

After that, every time I went downtown, I went over and chatted with Bobbie. She always acted very friendly, perhaps hoping I'd buy another subscription. She said she had a boyfriend, but she always acted like she'd like to get rid of him. But we never did date. And, of course, despite saving a receipt, I never did get my subscription to Florida Speaks Sportsman.

Some of the soldiers at Fort Bliss spent a lot of time in Mexico, since we were right on the border. Some of the places there were pretty crude, featuring risqué shows, prostitution and other things for the American guys. I don't want to get too graphic. Let me put it this way: They had sideshows with women who laid eggs on stage, in addition to a lot of other things.

I only crossed the border a couple of times. I had learned that, if you got in trouble for any reason at all, the Mexican cops could throw you in jail and might keep you for two weeks and never notify the U.S. authorities that you were there. When they finally notified them, you were Away Without Leave, or AWOL, and it didn't necessarily have to be your fault.

I made a trip one time to Truth or Consequences, New Mexico, for the wedding of one of my buddies. A group of us packed into an automobile to make the trip. The bride and her parents had come to New Mexico from up North, and the wedding was very small but romantic.

Afterward, we went to a dance at a bar in the city, only to find that you had to be 21 years of age to get in the place. In New York State at that time, 18 was the legal drinking age. We all felt that, if we could fight and die for our country, we should be able to legally drink a beer or two. There were a lot of good-looking girls at the bar and a lot of tough-looking cowboys, so it is probably just as well that we weren't allowed in. We might not have gotten safely out.

All through this time I kept in touch with folks back home with letters. I received a few from Carol LaPlante, and I wrote back, but Sally Christy was the one who wrote to me most regularly.

My sister, Jean, and six other girls from Norwood-Norfolk schools edited a little newsletter, "Your Friends," which they sent to all the local GIs in the service to tell us what was going on at home. Toward the back pages they had all the up-to-date addresses of everybody. They also had a place where they posted notes from the GIs.

I pose in my uniform during a visit to Norwood in September 1951. I gave this photo to Carol LaPlante. On the back I wrote, "Carol, All my love. Ken."

Here's one submission from me for the January 1951 newsletter:

Kenny LaRue, Norwood: I received another issue of the newspaper today and was more than pleased with it. I noticed that you corrected the error about George Harris. He had eighteen days at first but they got his clearance papers mixed up so he only got four days. He stayed for about three and a half days at Biggs Air Force Base waiting for a ride to New York, which never came. My advice to any guy who intends to rely on a hop is to go home by bus or train and not rely on a (military transport) hop. The paper was very good this time. The excerpts were exceptional. I really like to see what the other fellows have to say.

My Long Trip Back Home

Late in August 1951, I wrapped up radar school and got my orders to report to Fort Lawton in the state of Washington no later than September 13. Fort Lawton was where the Army was processing guys being sent overseas. I knew there was a possibility I would end up in Korea repairing radars.

I had been in the service for more than a year, and the Army owed me 30 days of leave. Instead, they told me I had what the military called a "nine days delay en route." That meant I could leave Texas and arrive in Seattle, Washington, in nine days instead of one. That gave me about a week at home before reporting.

Fortunately, I had been saving so I could afford to fly and get there quicker than riding a bus or train. I bought a ticket on American Airlines to Syracuse for $128.63, with stops in Dallas and Chicago.

Just out of Chicago, everything seemed to be going smoothly until the captain reported engine trouble. We had to return to Chicago and get another plane, which caused a delay of several hours. By the time I got to Syracuse, it was too late to catch a bus all the way to Norwood. I ended up on a bus going only as far north as Watertown, then started hitchhiking with my duffel bag. After a few miles, a couple picked me up in Evans Mills. Because I was a soldier, they took me past their hometown of Gouverneur all the way to Canton. I took a cab the final 15 miles or so home.

Having been gone for more than a year and knowing I might be destined for Korea, I decided to have a good old time and party as much as possible. I happened to see Carol LaPlante at a dance and I said hello. But during that entire week, I didn't once contact Sally Christy to let her know I was home.

Snubbing Sally was an awful thing to do, as she in theory was still my girlfriend and had been writing me faithfully for the past year. But at the time, I had too many opportunities to date. My attitude was, "I'm not ready to settle down. I'm having too much fun. Don't let somebody tie me down." Avoiding her seemed like the right thing to do at the time. Needless to say, she did not write to me after that. Over the years, I came to regret the decision and would sometimes wonder what I passed up.

I spent an extra day in Norwood before heading out. This meant I was going to arrive late at Fort Lawton, risking punishment for being AWOL. My attitude was the Army owed me the extra leave. I decided to take my chances.

I did not tell my parents I could be heading for Korea, but I think they figured it out. When I left, Mom stayed home and endured our goodbyes there. Dad took me to the bus station for the ride to Syracuse. For the first time in my life, I saw tears streaming down his face. It made it very hard to control my own emotions.

Later that day, I sent a postcard.

September 10, 1951

Mom,

Arrived in Syracuse OK. Leave at 9:35 tonight. Lots of love to all of you. I miss you already.

Ken

CHAPTER 3: Slow Boat to Japan

On September 11, I arrived at Fort Lawton in Washington and immediately ran into trouble. The corporal who signed me in looked at my papers then at me.

"Why are you late?"

"Well, I got screwed on my travel," I said.

Everyone in the military knew about the unreliability of American air travel in the early 1950s, so my excuse made sense. And it really didn't matter I was a day late. I still had lots of time before the ship left for the Far East. The corporal grumbled some more, but to my relief he eventually signed me in.

When I boarded the U.S.S. General Meigs on September 21, I couldn't believe its size. This was a transport ship about the length of two football fields. It had room to carry 5,200 GIs as well as a crew of about 600 or 700 on our 11-day voyage. The Meigs was named after a Civil War general who was key to the Union victory.

As soon as the ship got out of Puget Sound and into open water heading toward Japan, it began a slow rolling motion. I could feel my breakfast stir in my stomach. I'd heard from a buddy that a remedy for seasickness was to tighten the muscles of my stomach. He was right. Almost immediately I felt the queasiness ease. I kept my stomach tightened the whole voyage and I never felt sick again.

The U.S.S. General Meigs is seen in a Navy photo after the ship joined the Military Sea Transportation Service in July 1950. Photo courtesy of U.S. Naval Historical Center.

However, there were plenty of others who had trouble keeping down their meals. The railings were soon lined with guys throwing up their guts. The ship also placed 55-gallon drums in every section of the ship in case a soldier had to puke. Those quickly filled up with the vilest of liquids. Thank heaven I never was among the soldiers assigned to empty them overboard, or I would have been sick, stomach tightened or not.

We weren't long into the voyage when someone yelled, "Look, whales!" And, sure enough, there were a bunch of them swimming right beside the ship, probably out 500 to 600 feet. They followed right along with the ship for many, many miles.

The naval crew managed to give us three meals a day, although the lines were so long we spent more time standing in them than actually eating. In between meals and sleeping, we played cards and watched movies. Occasionally while we were seated on the floor in the indoor theater, the ship would list from side to side, and everyone would slide across the floor in one clump of bodies.

September 28, 1951

Dear Mom,

Here's your son again. I am now out at sea on my way to Japan. This is the seventh day at sea and the first chance I have had to write. Well, after I wrote you last, I was quickly processed and put on this ship on September 21. We left that night.

The quarters on the ship are awfully crowded. My bunk consists of a piece of canvas on a metal frame, and the bunk on top of mine is just about a foot above me, which makes it very difficult to climb into.

The first day out it was quite rough. Many of the guys were sick. I wasn't sick, but I was a little dizzy. The second day out we saw about 10 whales out about half a mile from the ship. Since then I have seen about 10 more whales, two sharks and some porpoises.

Five of my buddies from radar school are on the

ship. They are not in my compartment, but we see each other every day.

I haven't gotten a letter from any of you yet because I left Fort Lawton too quick and we don't have mail call aboard ship. That is one reason why I'll be glad to get over there.

How is everyone? Tell Dad, Jean, Ronny and Joe that I miss them and for them to write often. I miss you an awful lot, too, Mom, and I know you will write. That's why you're my best girl, because I know Mom is one girl who is always faithful.

I will write some more of this letter each day until I reach Japan, and then mail it there. I'm going to put it up for tonight and go shave and shower. I will write tomorrow again.

Because I couldn't send out mail on the ship, I just kept writing home one big long letter that I updated several times during the voyage.

September 30, 1951

Well, here I am again. Today has been quite a windy, rough day. The boat is rocking to beat all hell. So I'll think nothing of it if you can't read my writing.

Tell Dad, Jean, Ronny and Joe this letter is intended for them, too. I will write each of you separately as soon as I get settled. I really have list of people to write to.

If you can, I'd appreciate it if you would get the following addresses: Bob Steenberg, Punchy Palmer, Louie Stanford, Tommy Wheeland and Don Feickert. If Dick Kingsley and Glenn Young went in the Air Force, I would also like their addresses. I'm asking for a whole lot of stuff right now. That is just because I am getting settled over again.

I will close again for now and write again tomorrow.

Pee at Your Own Risk

The Meigs was a relatively modern ship – it was launched for service during the late part of World War II – but it had one big structural flaw that became clear when we ran into a pretty big storm. The porcelain urinals were troughs about 15 feet long and located in the front of the ship on the bottom level. The ship kept a steady flow of sea water pumped through them.

During the storm, the bow would go way up and then way down. And when it did, the sea water and everything else inside those urinals would hit the ceiling and rain back down. If you wanted to go to the bathroom – and you had to sooner or later – you had to get wet. And sometimes it was your own stuff that would come raining down on you.

I wouldn't even use the urinals if someone else was going. I'd wait until he got out. Then I'd run in, pee as fast as I could, and race out. But you couldn't help getting wet by a certain amount. It was a relief more ways than one when the storm finally subsided after about a day.

I spent a lot of time during the voyage playing cards with radar school classmate Ralph L. James Jr. He was tall, with a little mustache and rimless glasses. He was a nice-looking man who appeared a little older than the rest of us, who were mostly teenagers.

Ralph and I played hearts every single day during the voyage, and we shot the breeze a lot. It really made the time go by. We would also point out to each other whenever we saw whales or flying fish, or Japanese fishing ships when we got a little closer to the port of Yokohama.

October 1, 1951

Well, here I am again. If this keeps up, I will be writing a book. Today we found out positively that our destination is Yokohama, Japan. We should be there in about two more days as we are only 785 miles out from there now.

We passed a Japanese fishing boat today. It is the first boat we passed since we have been at sea. It caused quite a commotion because 5,000 guys were trying to get a look at it off the rail all at the same time.

If and when you have time, or if Jean has time, I would appreciate it if you could get a box, wooden or metal about the right shape and size, to put all my records and receipts in. And then if you can, put in all of my records, such as my yearbook, graduation certificates, honor certificates from high school and radar school, my insurance receipts, which I think I left at home, and anything else I send you from time to time. That way I can send you all my records and receipts, and any time I want something I can send for it and you will know where it is immediately and nothing will get torn or lost.

From time to time I will send you things, such as records of promotion (I hope), and some negatives of pictures I have taken. Any time I send negatives, you can get prints from those that you want to and then put them in the file. If you would do this, you would be doing me a big favor as I always would know my records are safe. You can put my birth certificate in with the other records and certificates.

In this letter, I am going to send you $50, which is the start of my new bank account. Either way, how much do I have since the allotments came? What I mean is, counting the money I'm sending you now, how much will I have at the end of October? I like to count my money and figure how much I can save before my next furlough. It gives me something to do.

Each month I will send you as much money as I can. I will send the $25 allotment plus $25 every month. The government now pays for our insurance, so I will draw $6.50 more each month, plus $8 for overseas pay. That is, if I stay a private. With my schooling, I should make corporal or sergeant soon, and I should be able to send much more each month. I plan to save enough so that when I get back to the States, I can fly home and have enough money to spend while I am home and to fly back.

I may buy myself a camera and some film in the PX tonight. There's a lot of interesting things to photograph around here. I think I shall make that my one hobby while I'm overseas, besides writing letters.

I will be awfully glad to get into a regular outfit where I can start getting some mail. That's the one thing I miss an awful lot besides being home.

How are Ronny and Joe doing in school? ... What grade is Joe in this year? Third or fourth?

I think Jean is making a big mistake by not going to college this year. If she doesn't go now, she will just keep postponing it and never go.

Well, until tomorrow I will close with my best wishes to all of you.

As nervous as I was about what lie ahead, I was thoroughly excited when we arrived in Japan on October 3. Everything about the country seemed exotic and wrapped in history. Looking down at the harbor from the ship, I noticed a wooden wharf with lots of Japanese busy. And with the nation still under American occupation, there was a certain amount of MPs around, too.

We waited on the ship several hours after we docked. Then all of a sudden, just like that, we were told to grab our bags and away we went down this long, sloping gangplank to the pier.

The Army put us in groups and marched us to this passenger train. It was a narrow gauge railway with tiny cars and a small engine, which I would discover was common for Japan.

From Yokohama, we traveled north near Tokyo to Camp Drake, which was the main replacement depot for American troops in Japan. The thing I noticed right away at Camp Drake was a water tower impressively painted with a giant yellow and black horse emblem of the 1st Cavalry Division. The division had left for fighting in Korea the previous year, but nobody took down that emblem, perhaps thinking they'd return soon.

October 4, 1951

So long, Mom, I'm in Japan and am too busy now to write more. I am safe and smiling. Got your letters, and I am not sending the $50 in this letter.

Love, Ken

I recall the three days I spent at Camp Drake, waiting for processing, as being dark and dismal. I don't recall seeing the sun much at all.

One other thing I remember – it's amazing what sticks in your mind all these years – was these young women trying to proposition guys for money from the other side of the camp fence. In a couple of cases, a guy would actually have her commit a sexual act right through the fence.

I had time to visit nearby Tokyo, which was a fascinating place. The city hadn't yet fully recovered from being fire-stormed in 1945 when it was practically burned to the ground by U.S. bombers. A lot of what you saw were wooden buildings that had fresh, unpainted lumber.

It was still an occupied country, but for the most part the people seemed subdued around those from the U.S. military. I didn't see anybody who looked angry when they saw us. They just went about their business.

At Camp Drake, I finally got my assignment: I was joining the 1st Cavalry Division's artillery battalion. All my buddies from radar school traveling on the Meigs got assigned to units based in Japan; I was the only darn one who was told he would join a unit then in Korea. The 1st Cavalry Division needed a radar repairman because the other one was getting close to the time to go home. Why I was picked to replace him, I don't know. Some clerk probably went eeny, meeny, miny, moe, and I was it.

Through Hiroshima, Nagasaki

I began my journey to Korea by taking a train out of Tokyo that was heading to Sasebo on the island of Honshu on the very southwestern tip of the country. Sasebo was best known then as the location of the largest of the Japanese naval bases during World War II.

I enjoyed looking out the window as we traveled along the coast, a few hundred feet from the sea. If we had derailed, we probably would have gone right into the ocean. The train also had the odd look of something right out of a "Looney Tunes" cartoon, with smaller cars than those in the United States.

The scenery in Japan was gorgeous. In 1951, Japan was still a quaint place in many ways with a traditionally Asian look. Many of the houses had thatched hut roofs. But there was also so much fresh construction with a lot of unpainted wood, just as I saw in Tokyo. Six years since the end of the war, Japan had not yet experienced the industrial revolution that would eventually make it a world economic powerhouse.

Every 30 minutes or so, everything went dark as our train went through long tunnels that cut through the hills.

October 8, 1951

Dear Mom,

Well, here I am again. I am on the train right now on the way to Sasebo, Japan, right down on the southern tip. We passed Mount Fujiyama this morning. It was a clear morning, so I got a really good look at it. It's awfully high.

We are supposed to pass through Hiroshima tomorrow morning. I want to see that.

If my writing is difficult to read, it's just because I am on the train. The little Jap trains rumble and shake like hellfire.

We went through many small villages this morning. We passed Shinto temples, mountains, etc. It has been dismal but I wouldn't have missed it for anything. The amazing thing here is the agriculture. No matter where you go, every small bit of land is farmed. On the edge of a forest, the vegetables and rice are planted right next to the trees, right up next to the railroad tracks. I suppose the reason for this is because they have so many people.

We just went by a Buddhist temple. It has a big Buddhist statue on a mountaintop. Some of these tunnels in the mountains are really long. We went through one this morning, which must have been two miles long. We got inside and it's dark as night.

And all the villages we passed, the people stand outside and watch us go by. Some of the kids at the stops come up beside the train begging for cigarettes and candy.

How are Dad, Jean, Ronny and Joe? All fine here. I hope you, too.

Please disregard the 1st Cavalry address I gave you because I am not sure that it is the correct one, and I don't want any of my mail to be sidetracked.

We had chicken for lunch today. It was pretty good. It is awfully hard to eat on the train without spilling food or coffee all over yourself. The train conductor just told me that we won't reach Hiroshima until about 10 o'clock tonight, so I probably won't see much of it.

It won't be long now before all my mail will be free. Also, if Korea is affected by the GI Bill, I will get that.

We switched to a sleeper this morning. It isn't much like an American sleeper, but we do have beds. Whenever I get the chance, I don't know when that will be, I will send Dad and the kids each a 1st Cavalry shoulder patch.

I just found out also we go through Nagasaki on our trip. We will go through there about 12 noon tomorrow.

If you do not hear from me as often as you used to, remember that it's because I may not have time or stationery.

Morale over there is more important than ever before. So make Dad, Jean and the kids write often. Set up a standing rule in the house that they have to write at least once a week. That way I shall hear from them even though I don't have time to write back.

How are the two squirts? I suppose they are both busy every day in school. How is the old boy? Tell him to write often, too. Does Jean still kiss his bald spot? Wait until he sees my new patch. It is about the largest patch the army has.

I miss you an awful lot, too, Mom. One thing, however, I will be home a lot quicker this way than had I stayed in Japan or Okinawa. So long for now.

You may not hear from me again right off, although I will write as often as possible.

Give my love to all. God bless you, Mom.

Love, Ken

I was disappointed that it was nighttime when we passed through Hiroshima. We really couldn't see rebuilding underway at the place flattened by the first atomic bomb dropped on a city. But it was daylight when we passed through the second atomic bomb target, Nagasaki. There were lots of signs of devastation, with more wood that hadn't had time to age.

On our journey, we often stopped at railroad stations. I went into one to use the toilet and discovered that it was one big john in a room for everybody. I sat on a toilet, and a woman sat right next to me with no divider. I did my business and got out of there as quickly as I could.

Wherever I went in Japan, the native women were quite attractive for the most part, which a young guy always notices.

I spent a lot of time on the train talking to a Korean War veteran traveling with us. He had been wounded in action and sent to a hospital in Japan. He was now shipping back to his outfit because he was healed. I don't remember his name, but he was a real sociable guy. I picked his brain all the way to Korea about what it was like and what I should do if I got up there and I was on the line. For example, he talked about the importance of not giving the enemy easy targets by "bunching up" with other soldiers.

I chatted with him for hour after hour. I think he was glad to talk, because he didn't mind bragging a little bit about being in combat. And I was a good listener, in a self-preservation sort of way.

In Sasebo, we got off the train and marched onto a little Japanese freighter. It looked like something from the 1800s, all wood with straw mats on the floor. There were porcelain circles surrounding holes in the deck, over which we were expected to squat to relieve ourselves.

Fortunately, we weren't awfully long on that ship. We left Japan sometime in the morning and by afternoon on October 10 we were in Korea, landing at Pusan Harbor. As we peered down from the ship, a little band of American troops played the 1950 hit novelty song, "If I Knew You Were Comin' I'd've Baked a Cake." I've hated that song ever since.

CHAPTER 4: The Jamestown Line

Once off the ship in South Korea, I was driven by the Army to a camp built up high over Pusan. There I waited for my new assignment, getting a good vantage point of the devastation. It was a pretty ragged-looking city because there was a war on. There were a lot of damaged and destroyed buildings. You could see huts for refugees who had flocked to the southeastern corner of the peninsula after the North Koreans invaded.

But it was the sight of the beggar children that stuck with me most. I had time to go outside to look around. Along the wire fence, dozens of children in filthy rags waited for soldiers. Most of the youngsters were begging for cigarettes, candy, money, food, anything really. I'd throw them a cigarette just to see what they'd do. Some guys threw whole packs. I didn't. I relied on my cigarettes. I also threw the children a little candy. After a while I noticed the youngsters never ate the candy or smoked the cigarettes. They brought them over to some adult in the distance, then ran back and begged for more.

October 10, 1951

Dear Mom,

I arrived in Pusan approximately 7 o'clock this morning aboard a Japanese transport. We had coffee at the docks, and moved up to a replacement company overlooking Pusan Harbor. It is quite warm here, but in the city itself it is extremely overcrowded with refugees. The whole place is filthy and stinky. You don't dare go downtown for fear you will be contaminated.

The kids come up to the fences just around our camp and beg and steal or sell whatever they can. They are extremely dirty, malformed and all covered with scars.

The terrain, although this may seem impossible, is all hills. You either live on one side of the hill or the other, or in between the hills. It is like looking at the moon with no vegetation and black ridges all around.

Well, there's a description of Pusan for you. It's a typical war-ridden town. There's a bunch of North Korean prisoners of war working inside the post. They have such innocent looks that you feel sorry for them, until you remember the SOBs probably killed plenty of our GIs before they were captured.

It isn't a pretty sight here, Mom. It makes you appreciate the good old USA more than ever. Our slums of any city we have would be mansions over here.

I have been writing long letters every time I write because I can't write as often as I did. I'm going to write Grandma as soon as I can. Tell her I said that I was thinking of her.

I just don't seem to have time to write to the whole family, so please read this to all the rest. I will write them whenever I can. Tell them not to wait until hearing from me before they write. I haven't had any mail in about five days now, but that's because there hasn't been any mail call.

Up here, you don't have to shave anymore. After I get further north, there is no more saluting or anything like that.

Well, Mom all my love to you, Dad, Jean, Ronny and Joe.

Love,
Ken

Regrettably this is the last known letter of mine to survive from my time in Korea. But I still own a small notebook in which I scratched the dates of key events in the weeks ahead. In Pusan, I was eager to finally begin duties as a radar repairman.

By this time, as peace talks continued, both sides locked into fierce battles to claim hills near the 38th Parallel and to put pressure on the other side to negotiate more favorable terms. The war continued to pile up casualties on both sides, although by one estimate the Chinese suffered 10 times as many killed as did U.S. forces.

I wasn't in Pusan too long before the Army loaded a large group of us onto a train and shipped us north.

During the long ride, all of the train windows were completely boarded up to prevent the enemy from tossing grenades inside as we passed. We went through Taegu and Taejon, and then swung west just south of Seoul.

A God Awful Sound

We finally arrived at the replacement depot, or "repo depot," at a place called Uijeongbu (pronounced Wee John Boo). From there I was sent to the 1st Cavalry Division Artillery Headquarters Battery, arriving October 12, 1951. After 14 months in the Army, I finally belonged to a unit.

When I reported to the captain, I was told that the man I was replacing was in the field repairing radar, so there really wasn't any radar work for me to do until he got back. Over the next week, I joined other newcomers receiving a crash course in conditioning by running up and down the hills. I spent a few hours being shown the right way to dig a fox hole and to keep rain out by covering it with a poncho.

The artillery headquarters was out in the open with a bunch of tents to sleep in, but there were also trenches and heavy guard duty at night in case of attack. Everyone seemed very nervous. We were maybe 10 or 15 miles behind the front. Still, I could hear this God awful sound just north of us, like distant thunder that never ended. It was just explosions and explosions and explosions. You could hear *boom-da-boom-da-boom* constantly. It was obvious that a big battle was taking place.

I was at headquarters for a week before Captain Patrick J. Troy called me and two other newcomers into a tent. He got right to the point.

"I'm sorry to tell you this, but I'm shipping you up to the front," he said quietly.

He told me I was being assigned as an infantryman with the 1st Cavalry Division's 2nd Battalion, 8th Cavalry Regiment.

I was stunned. "Sir," I said, "I just spent 11 months in radar repair and maintenance school. I'm a radar repairman." It seemed to me like an awful waste of an education to put me under daily enemy fire.

Captain Troy nodded sympathetically.

"I'll tell you what. I've thought about this long and hard," he said. "As you know there have been a lot of casualties on the front. They've ask us to send up every spare person in the outfit. Well, I just can't part with any of the guys that I know. I've gotten close to them. Because I don't know you, I'm going to send you and these two other fellows, because that's the only way I can handle it."

I didn't try to argue further. The captain was extraordinarily nice about it, and his logic made some sense: I was a soldier first and a technician second.

So next thing I knew I was in a jeep riding another dirt road, carrying my M-1, and holding onto a duffel bag stuffed with my gear and a few personal belongings. I wasn't carrying a lot. I had a few extra clothes, a new watch, a camera and my shaving outfit in a bag. I also had some letters from home that I stored in a little box.

We traveled through Seoul, the capital of South Korea. There weren't many buildings in the entire city that hadn't been destroyed. We crossed the Han River north of the city and drove north of Yonchon until I arrived at the front, technically known as the Main Line of Resistance (MLR). The Army called the current position the Jamestown Line.

I looked around. Our section of the line was a series of sharp hills, some hundreds of feet high with very sharp drops on the backside to the south and sloping gradually toward the enemy line to the north. In front of us was a huge valley studded with isolated hills in the center. Directly in front of us, behind a line of barbed wire, were minefields that any enemy would have to go through to reach us.

Someone told me to try to keep my steel helmet on at all times because we never knew when an attack could come.

I spent a couple of days doing patrol training and being prepared for the line before the 8th Cavalry sent me to G Company, or George Company as it was typically called. We were right next to F Company, also known as Fox Company. Each company consisted of about 150 men in three platoons, plus some support troops operating heavier guns.

Each platoon was composed of four squads of about 10 men. My squad was led by Cpl. Newton "Steve" Babcock, who was from Framingham, Massachusetts. He was a bit older than the rest and carried himself with a manner that seemed more mature than most guys. He immediately impressed me.

Life in the Trenches

Babcock showed me the trenches on top of our assigned hill, right next to an even taller one known as Bloody Baldy. It got the name from the soldiers because the fighting and shelling had all but stripped it of most vegetation. The hill overlooked the Imjin River not far from Sonybok.

At night, I slept in a small hilltop trench with two other soldiers squeezed next to me. While two slept, the third was on guard duty for three hours. When his time was up, another would take over watching for the enemy while others slept.

Standing guard was especially nerve-wracking, because you had to be on the constant lookout in the dark. The enemy was mainly Chinese, and when I was there they only attacked at night. They knew if they attacked in the daytime, they would just get slaughtered by our superior weaponry.

Earlier in the war, the Chinese did attack during the day with human waves. They would come at U.N. Forces with thousands of soldiers in hopes our troops couldn't kill them as fast as they could send them. Sometimes, the Chinese would send their people right through our mine fields, knowing ones that died first would clear a spot for the ones behind them. They had men with pistols, Communist officers, who came along behind. If one of their soldiers didn't go along and do what they were told, they were shot right there. A lot of their soldiers weren't even armed with rifles. They just had baskets of wooden potato masher grenades.

Eventually, the casualties must have been too high even for the Chinese leaders, and they resorted to sneak attacks at night.

On October 29, the captain sent several of us to the front of our hill to stretch out two more rows of barbed wire on metal posts. Before we started, the captain warned us not to "bunch up" in groups and make ourselves an easier target..

All of a sudden, I heard the *boom-boom-boom-boom* of

artillery.

"Get down!" someone yelled.

The experienced guys immediately dove for a low spot. Around me, though, there were no holes or even a depression. I fell on my stomach, hands over my head, as shells swished above me and exploded several feet away. They came damn awful close, or so it seemed at the time.

When the firing stopped, I jumped to my feet and raced toward the nearest trench. As I stepped over a row of barbed wire, I heard cloth being ripped. Once safely in a trench, I looked down to see a long tear in my khaki pants, from my crotch to the bottom of the right leg. Miraculously, the barbed wire didn't cut skin. I found some old phone wire and wrapped it around my leg to close up my pants the best I could.

A little while later, Babcock handed me a Combat Infantry Badge, which is given automatically to an infantry soldier who is under fire.

"Well, you certainly earned that today," he said.

Of all military awards I received, I am most proud of this one. I pinned the badge to my shirt, but I didn't do anything more about my pants for about a week. Finally, the chill below overcame my embarrassment. After I mentioned my torn pants to an officer, he got me another pair right away.

Not long after arriving at the front, I was promoted to private first class. I was glad to get it, but I still felt I deserved to be a corporal or even a sergeant at that point because of all my time in the service. But I kept this beef mostly to myself.

CHAPTER 5: I Was a Teenage B.A.R. Man

Living outside 24 hours a day on the Jamestown Line meant a lot of us were hungry 24 hours a day. We got our Army meals. But we had no local corner store to go to for extra food, so we were constantly obsessed with eating.

The photo is a bit muddy, but that's me on the left reading a comic book along the Jamestown Line. Just to the right of that big tree in the middle is squad leader Steve Babcock, bent over working on our little portable gas stove.

We sat in the trenches at night describing our perfect meal, the one we would have when we got home. "Macaroni with tomatoes," I would tell my buddies about a favorite meal I made with my sister while our parents were away. "I cannot wait to get home to eat macaroni and tomatoes." The guys laughed, except their fantasies were just as personal. Those who were worldlier described meals that a small-town boy like me never knew: Maybe an appetizer of steamed oysters, an entree of foie gras, or a dessert of crème brûlée.

On the front, we got hot food just once a day, served at the foot of the hill. The cooks dished the food from heated cases right into our mess gear, which was an aluminum, two-part device. It had two deep plates, one with dividers, fastened together. I couldn't wait each day for the hot chow, but it took every bit of agility I had to get down our steep hill. As the snow came and it really got slippery, I could only get down safely by hanging onto a tree limb or anything else I could find along the way.

The rest of our meals were cold rations: boxes filled with cans of food, chocolate, coffee, crackers, etc. Occasionally, the Army also sent up candy bars. On rare occasions, they even sent us a couple of bottles of beer each.

We had one little stove that heated all the water for coffee and everything, and squad leader Babcock took care of that. It used gas, and he had to pump it to get it to work.

In addition to the food, the Army sent up cigarettes every day. Everyone got them, whether they smoked or not. At the time I smoked quite a bit, so some of my nonsmoking buddies gave me theirs in trades.

I got mail regularly on the front, and I sent letters home without confirming I was on the front line. They were already worried enough to know I was in Korea. Mostly, I wrote home asking Mom for food. I told her that I had three meals a day and that was it. I would say something like, "I'm always hungry because I'm outside all the time, never inside. If you could send me some stuff like canned soups, powdered coffee, sugar, creamer and ..." I went on and made a whole long list of what I would like. I asked her to pay for it from my bank account, although I don't think she ever did.

I also asked Mom to send me a few books. I spent a lot of time reading whatever I could find. I have a somewhat blurry photo showing me reading a comic book on a hill behind the front line.

This all might sound like a grand camping trip, but I tell you there was no forgetting it was war. The enemy shelled us every day. We shelled every day. I saw flaming napalm dropped from jets. Sometimes it got a little close to our positions, which is why we were taught to put ponchos over our trenches, as if that would keep napalm from spilling in. We had firefights where enemy bullets sounded like bees flying just over my head.

My training with the M1 paid off on the front. In basic, I learned to take that rifle apart and put it back together many times; now I could have done it in the dark. It wasn't that complicated to begin with, but I felt comfortable it would work if I needed it.

The Browning Automatic Rifle

One day Steve Babcock told me I was the squad's new "B.A.R. Man," which meant duty handling a Browning Automatic Rifle. The Browning fired the same ammo that an M1 rifle used, but we could set it for automatic fire and it would shoot a whole bunch of bullets at once. But unless the enemy was getting close and we needed to clean them out in a hurry, I usually fired single shots with the B.A.R. It was very accurate single shot, as accurate as an M1. Up close you could easily drill the enemy right in the head.

Some guys with the B.A.R. got excited and they just sprayed, sprayed, sprayed bullets with it. They were lucky if they got one or two people with that ham-handed approach. But if you took your time and aimed, you got somebody every time you fired.

I liked the B.A.R., except it was damn awful heavy to carry. I think it weighed about 16 pounds. I had an assistant B.A.R. Man who came along with me. He carried my extra ammo, because a soldier shot a lot of ammo with a B.A.R. I also had a vest to store extra ammo. The other downside to being a B.A.R. Man is that it put me in more danger. The enemy was more likely to target a B.A.R. Man because it knew he was carrying a weapon that was so much more deadly.

The enemy had its own rapid fire guns – what we called burp guns. They could spray 20 bullets a second at you. But they weren't as good as our Brownings.

Waiting for the Enemy

Our constant fear was that the enemy would infiltrate our lines at night and stab us to death as we slept. One night, we heard a snap behind the fence and spotted this figure huddled in the darkness. He was just a boy. We thought at first he was a defector, but upon questioning, we discovered he was a spy.

We also had to keep a lookout for Washing Machine Charlie, an enemy pilot who flew an old biplane at night. If he saw a light, he'd fly right over it and drop a grenade or whatever. He never really did much damage because he made so much noise when he was approaching, like a clunky old washing machine. You learned to cover any light when you heard him.

One dreaded job on the Jamestown Line was patrol duty. Every few days, our platoon was sent out in front of the line, in full sight of the Chinese across the valley, to probe as far as we could. The idea was to lure the enemy soldiers into confirming their location. When they started shooting at us, we'd turn around and come back. But we had to keep going until they shot at us, or until one of our officers with binoculars saw they were beginning to get ready to shoot. Most often, long before we got even half way to its line, the enemy would send artillery shells our way in order to deter us from going on any further. The fire was never very accurate. If they hit us, it was due to dumb luck, not their accuracy.

On my very first patrol, we marched in a long line maybe 20 feet apart with a telephone-style line trailing us back to the officers. (We couldn't count on walkie-talkies because the enemy sometimes jammed the signals, or even gave orders over them in perfect English.)

On these patrols, we were very vulnerable because the enemy was hiding and we were the ones who were out in the open, not in our fortified trenches. The enemy might be ahead of us or it could be behind us. We always had one or two soldiers in the rear who were walking backward and watching our behinds all the time.

I quickly picked up the habit of constantly looking for any depression I could see along the road in case we came under fire. I would then dive into that spot. Unless the shell hit right on me, I would be okay because the shrapnel would fly up in a cone shape and miss striking anyone in a low spot on the ground.

I tried to be careful about keeping 20 feet away from the next person. Some guys, though, were dumber than a bunch of rocks. Although we were warned over and over not to do it, a few on my first patrol started bunching up. I guess human nature causes men in danger to feel safer when they are closer together.

Sure enough, the enemy started firing shells. *Boom-boom-boom-boom.* I dove for one of those depressions, and I stayed right there until the shelling stopped and we got the order to head back to our trenches.

On that first patrol, a couple of guys weren't so lucky. They didn't get hurt. But they managed to dive into fresh human excrement.

We Didn't Call It Pork Chop Hill

George Company's other main duty was manning our main outpost. The outpost was on a hill that came up in the middle of the valley in front of the Jamestown Line. The hill had a peak at the center, with three ridges running away from it, one on each side and one toward the enemy. The Army referred to it as Hill 255. Some soldiers called it Three Sisters, although I knew it only as "the outpost."

Years later, I would learn that U.S. troops fighting there later gave it a different name: Pork Chop Hill. This was presumably because the hill had a shape somewhat like a pork chop. "Pork Chop Hill," a book and movie of the same name, told of the horrifying and meaningless fighting there months after the 1st Cavalry rotated out.

I think our whole platoon had to go out there once a week, living around the clock for two days, just 500 feet away from the Chinese.

This is the top of the 8th Cavalry outpost on Hill 255, not far from enemy lines. The outpost had a big trench with sandbags.

The purpose of the outpost was to be close enough to the enemy that we could see what they were doing, and we could also be close enough to them that they couldn't just sneak up to our Main Line of Resistance without being seen. They would have to take that outpost before an attack on the line.

Hill 255 had this big circular trench around it, all behind barbed wire. Each of the three ridges had its own small hole, each about 3 feet deep. The officers would post two men in each of the small holes to act as an early warning of attack on the outpost. Those of us in the holes had a telephone line back to the outpost to communicate if we saw anything.

One chilly night in November, the captain assigned me and another guy to the western hole and two others to the hole on the eastern side. Each of us had an M1 rifle and extra ammo. If the enemy showed up, we were supposed to shoot them, or else get the hell out of there.

I hated that assignment. We were outside the barbed wire at night just a few hundred feet from the enemy. The rest of our guys were up in a bunker in that nice outpost, at least it seemed nice at the time.

We were watching and watching. There was no moon, but there was enough light to see anything nearby.

I learned later that the two guys on the eastern side fell asleep. All of a sudden, a couple of Chinese soldiers poked them in the side and motioned for them to get out of the hole. They were going to take them prisoner.

One of the two Americans told the other quietly, "I am not going to be captured. I'm going to run for it. And in two seconds, I'm going to take off like a bat out of hell, yelling at the top of my lungs, and you come along with me."

"OK," the other guy said.

The Chinese were still pushing them when our two guys jumped out of their hole and ran toward the bunker, yelling to our platoon, "Don't shoot! Don't shoot! It's us! We're coming in! We were just captured by a couple of Chinese!"

Our guys let the two Americans in, then started shooting down where they had been. but the Chinese were long gone. I'm sure they ran like hell.

All through this, the two of us in our western hole kept our heads down.

After the shooting stopped, I rang up our landline telephone to the trench.

I asked the lieutenant, "What's going on?"

"Oh, nothing too bad," he said. "Just watch real close because the two guys on the other end almost got captured."

"Can we come in?"

"Yeah, you can come in."

"Be careful you don't shoot us, eh?"

"No, I'll give the orders not to fire."

We jumped out of our hole, yelling all the way. "We are coming in! Don't shoot! Don't shoot!"

Hiding in a Chinese Foxhole

On another night, three of us were sent to the foot of the outpost to crawl inside an old Chinese foxhole carved into the side of the hill. It was cleverly built, with a sudden turn inside that protected soldiers from exploding shells. We had to enter on hands and knees and wait there through the night, watching for the enemy.

About dusk, shelling started. For three or four hours,

thousands of shells exploded, some very near us. We sat huddled in the corner of the hole, expecting any moment that enemy soldiers would appear at the opening.

Being a moonlit night, it would have been easy for us to see them and for them to see us. Fortunately, it turned out that the enemy was attacking further down the line, and only wanted to keep us in our trenches and not outflanking their attack.

At daybreak, we crawled out, rather unsteady, and rejoined our outfit on top of the outpost. We saw where all the shells had landed near our hole. It was a bit unnerving knowing those were meant to kill us.

CHAPTER 6: Heroes, Cowards and Fools

The Army had a simple way of identifying the remains of a dead soldier. At all times, in all weather, in all situations, I had to wear around my neck a chain issued with two tiny metal dog tags. I was issued mine soon after I went in the service. They include my name, blood type (mine has a big O) and my Army serial number.

My two dog tags, showing their age and some wear from Army service.

There's also a notch in each of those dog tags. If I got killed in action, someone was supposed to pry my mouth open and use the notch to hook it into my teeth. That way, if my body wasn't discovered right away, it rotted or whatever, those dog tags would be firmly attached to help identify me.

Of course, I never arrived at the battlefield thinking my tags would be needed that way. When you're 19, you believe you're going to live forever. You're immortal – until something happens that brings you to the reality of the situation.

One of my first outpost duties occurred November 2, 1951. Our squad had just received a couple of replacements, including a soldier whose first name was Francis. He was from Kentucky and he was a giant of a guy. He must have been about 6-foot-4 and about 220 pounds. Of course, we all joked about how big of a target he was going to be for the Chinese. Francis was good-natured and laughed with the rest of us.

There wasn't much to do at the outpost that day except to keep an eye out for the enemy and to listen for any incoming shells.

I was seated on the backside of the hill, about 10 feet below the crest, when I heard that familiar *boom-boom-boom-boom*. I immediately dove toward a slit trench. It was only about a foot deep, but it was big enough to hold a person. I grabbed two sand bags, pulled one over my head and another over my backside.

The first shell hit on my side of the hill about 30 feet below me. The next one hit closer. I could tell what the enemy was doing. Their soldiers were just slightly adjusting the arc each time, so the shells kind of walked up the hill about 10 feet apart.

A third one exploded about 10 feet below me.

Oh, my God, I thought. *The next one is going to hit right on me.* I realized how much danger I was in, and I began praying.

I heard the next shell whirring in, but because of its slightly lower arc, it never reached me. Instead, it clipped the top of the hill, entering a very small opening in the bunker that was otherwise well-protected with logs and sandbags. The shell struck Francis in the head. Killed him instantly, and wounded another guy in the trench with him and two others about 20 feet away.

As the shelling continued, I heard someone call for the medic. The medic didn't move right away; it took several shouts from the captain for him to come out of his trench. If he had got going earlier, he might have been killed, too.

There was nothing anyone could do about Francis, I was told. I didn't go inside the bunker and look.

Most Heroes End Up Dead

In a little while, a group of young Korean men we called "choggie boys" came up to the outpost, loaded Francis' body onto a stretcher, wrapped it in a white rubber sheet and carried it off the hill. The Army tried to keep our soldiers from handling our dead because they knew it hurt morale.

When Francis' body went by me, his hand suddenly slipped out. It swung back and forth for several seconds, attached by a cord at the wrist.

"Get that son of a bitchin' hand back in there right away," the captain growled, and one of the boys grabbed the hand and put it back under the sheet and took the body away. That's last I saw of Francis.

Years later, I looked up his casualty file. Francis was a PFC, just 21 years old when he was killed. He was buried in Maplelawn Cemetery in Paducha, Kentucky.

I was not the only one who never forgot his death.

Another soldier from my squad, Bernard Heaney, wrote about it in 2010 at koreanwar.org. His recollections differ only whether it was the third or fourth shell that hit the bunker. "I was talking to (Francis) ... just before the rounds started coming in. I dove up the trench and he stayed in a partial finished bunker. The second shell collapsed the trench alongside me and the third hit the bunker. This was his first patrol."

John Krull, another member of George Company, wrote succinctly in 2009: "Francis spent only one night on the line, but I think of him often."

The other wounded were treated at the scene and then carried to ambulances and away back to Japan.

Francis' death really shook me up. It was the first time I had seen someone killed. After he got mangled like that, and so easily it could have been me, I wasn't so sure I was going to make it out alive. The longer I was there, the less I thought my chances were for surviving. With all those bullets and shells flying, I figured that the odds were that sooner or later they were going to get me.

But as time went on, I adjusted pretty quickly. The deep fear eased, and I just tried all I could to make sure I wasn't among the ones killed or wounded.

I'm sure I was like most soldiers in George Company or anywhere else who had to fight in a war: I followed orders. I fought as much as the next guy. But I wasn't trying to be a hero. I figured most heroes end up dead.

George Company did have a few of what I considered to be cowards. We had one guy who joined George Company the same time as me. When he got up on the line, he "accidentally" fell down the steep backside of our hill. He didn't fall head-first or anything, but he got part of the way down the hill and fell. He did that two or three times and they made him a cook. They moved him back 10 to 15 miles behind the line. He only had to come to the front to bring our hot chow.

We had another soldier who reported in sick just before we were sent out on a two-day patrol, so he stayed behind in our trench. Before long, he started falling down the hill. He must have seen how it worked for the other guy. Sure enough, they made him a cook. too.

Not Letting Sleeping Dogs Lie

Some others just didn't seem cut out for war. One guy in our squad, Frank, talked with a big-city, tough-guy accent, at least when he wasn't huffing and puffing. He was overweight and he smoked cigarettes and maybe even had emphysema. When he went on patrol, he would tire out a lot easier than the rest of us, but I'll give him credit for one thing: He hung with us.

One night, I was in a hole on the outpost with Frank and another guy. I took the first shift of guard duty from 9 to midnight. When my time was up, I gave Frank a nudge for him to take over while I got some sleep.

"Come on, Frank, time to get up," I said.

He didn't move or say anything. I knew he was awake because his snoring stopped, but he pretended he was asleep. I kept telling him to get up and kept nudging him with a little more force.

Eventually, I kicked him hard in the side with my boot.

"Ow!" he moaned, finally getting to his feet. "I'm getting up to kick the hell out of you."

"It's your shift," I told him quietly. I was too tired to argue, and he calmed down when he woke up a bit more. I zipped up my sleeping bag and went to sleep and he took guard duty for the next three hours, and that was it.

Our squad always had two or three guys with issues. Maybe that's because Steve Babcock was such a good squad leader. The officers knew they could give him difficult cases and he could make a soldier out of anyone.

One such guy was a PFC from Massachusetts. He was tall, very thin-faced and acted a little slow, maybe even slightly mentally retarded. Consequently some of the guys picked on him a bit. I'm sure the captain put him in our squad because he knew Steve would take good care of him. And Steve did, which is why this newcomer thought the world of our squad leader. Very quickly, the rest of us stopped picking on the guy because we really respected Steve and knew he wouldn't like it if we continued.

'Duck! There's a Grenade!'

Another soldier in our squad was anything but a coward. This PFC, who looked barely old enough to shave, was more gung-ho about combat than anyone I knew. He just loved it. He loved going on patrol and loved firing at the enemy. Of course, I don't think he had ever seen anybody killed or torn apart with a shell, so he was still very game.

One night, they transferred some of us over to a hill further up the line. This young guy was in the trench next to me. It was dark but too early to sleep. So I sat puffing on a cigarette and shooting the breeze and all that.

All of a sudden I heard *ping!* followed by the sound of something rolling in front of me down the hill.

"Duck! There's a grenade!" I yelled.

It exploded, and I heard its shrapnel hitting the trees. I knew it immediately wasn't an enemy grenade because it came from our direction.

I said, "Who in hell threw that grenade?"

A little voice came from the next trench.

"I did. I did. I'm sorry," our young PFC said. "I thought I heard something."

Well, I knew he didn't hear anything. He just wanted to throw the grenade because he got bored.

And I said, "Well, you know, you almost killed three guys."

"I'm sorry," he repeated meekly.

"If you throw another one of those friggin' grenades without there being something there, I'm going to come over there and shoot you."

"No, no, no. I won't do it again."

About a week later, his mother found out he was on the line in combat. It turned out that he enlisted at only 15 years old, and he was now just 16. The Army came up and got him and took him away and sent him home to be discharged. I would imagine, as soon as he got to be 17, he rejoined. He wanted that war more than anybody I ever saw. He always had a big smile. It was like he was in a kid's game.

Fortunately, we had our share of really good soldiers in our squad. Among them was Bernard Heaney, who was from Greenport, New York. He was a nice guy and a dependable soldier. He was the kind you felt would stay there and fight if things got bad. In recent years, we reconnected over the Internet and sent email back and forth. He's still a very nice guy.

Another excellent soldier and a good friend was Bob Schmelling of Manitoe, Michigan. He was short, stocky – very good-looking in the face. He had a kind of ruddy complexion and a big smile all the time. And he was always dependable when you were on the line.

John Pilla of Philadelphia, Pennsylvania, wasn't very tall – probably 5-2 or 5-3 – but he was a very handsome Italian with dark curly hair and a nice smile. The thing I remember most is that he could sing like nobody I ever heard before in person. He had the most beautiful voice. He sounded like a cross between Frank Sinatra and Dean Martin. Many a night on the line, he entertained us for hours. We would ask him to sing certain songs, and he knew them all the way through. He would sing until we got tired enough and wanted to go to sleep.

These were the good guys, all men who should be proud of their service. But one enlisted man among us stood out at the time: Cpl. Ralph Forkes, a short, stocky soldier from Hollywood, California.

Cpl. Ralph Forkes, my squad mate in Korea, here later as a beer buddy in Japan.

When I got to George Company, Ralph was already something of a legend. Weeks before, he was out with 2nd Platoon during a night patrol when our forces exchanged fire with the enemy. The B.A.R. Man guarding the rear was badly wounded, and several others were also hit. Most of our guys managed to escape and get back to where George Company was dug in along the line.

The next day, the platoon went back looking for its missing men. They found Ralph, who had pulled the B.A.R. Man into some brush and kept him quiet because there were a lot of Chinese still around. Ralph had barely survived the battle himself after he was hit in the forehead with a grenade that failed to explode. The platoon retrieved Ralph and the B.A.R. Man, and both survived the ordeal.

If there was a man among us who deserved a medal for heroism, we all agreed Ralph Forkes should have gotten it. But, as far as I knew, he never did.

CHAPTER 7: Prayers in the Foxhole

In early November, just a few days after Francis was killed, our platoon was sent to the outpost again. It was probably mid-afternoon when the enemy started to shell us. I heard that familiar *boom-boom-boom-boom*.

I immediately made a dive into a small trench. When I did, I accidentally put my hand onto an empty ammo can sitting in the dirt. The can was about 14 inches long with a sharp metal edge because the top had been cut off. The metal edge sliced my right palm, which began bleeding quite badly. The gash was just an inch or so from the scar from that firecracker that exploded in my hand when I was 5.

When the shelling stopped, there was one guy gravely wounded – someone from another squad – and two other guys with lesser injuries. They needed medical attention a lot more than I did. So, I grabbed something and wrapped it around my hand to stop the bleeding until the medic could get to me. The choggie boys soon arrived to pick up the wounded on stretchers and to haul them out. At that point, the badly wounded soldier was already dead.

About 20 minutes later, some of the guys noticed that I had an injured hand.

"Medic!" someone yelled. "LaRue is hurt."

The medic raced over. "What is it?"

I opened up my hand, and blood poured out.

"What happened?" he asked as he sprinkled some sulfa drug in there.

I explained that I cut myself diving on the ammo can when the shells came in.

He said nothing as he wrapped my hand with a fresh bandage, then he looked at me.

"You'll be fine," he said, then added: "I'll put you in for the Purple Heart."

The Purple Heart? I didn't think of that. That was something you get for taking a bullet or a piece of shrapnel fighting the enemy. I essentially was attacked by a Spam can.

"Don't do that," I said. "Don't put me in for the Purple Heart."

"You've earned it if you want it," he said.

"Thanks," I said. "But I have been praying every day that I would be able to eventually leave the front without being killed or injured. If I got a Purple Heart for an accident, even if it was in combat, then I wouldn't be faithful to the prayers I've been saying to keep me safe."

My fear was, if I took a Purple Heart I didn't really deserve, God wouldn't protect me any longer from being seriously hurt, if not killed. I didn't want a Purple Heart badly enough to test my theory of divine retribution.

The medic accepted my explanation and didn't put me in for the Purple Heart, and not a day goes by where I regret my decision.

My faith I lived daily on the front. But let's face it. It's easy to pray when you're on the battlefield. People who barely know God do it. It's just human nature when times are bad to turn to prayer, then forget about God when you think you're out of danger.

I knew I had another six months to go on the front before I would have enough time in to automatically move off the line, and I didn't know if I would make it. So it's not hard to pray every day when your life is at stake. But I believed in God since I was a child. I had always been a good churchgoer, even in busy times after I got in the service. I also knew my mother and father were praying every day for my safe return.

In Korea, when I knew the Army chaplain was on his way up, and that he was going to say Mass at 2 o'clock or whatever, I was always there. This happened to be a Catholic chaplain. He would hold the service at the bottom of the hill, on the backside out of view of the enemy, so we were fairly safe.

It was a simple service. He had a little stand there and he had the host and all that. It was a very portable thing he could set up. He did not waste a lot of time. If the Mass was 20 to 25 minutes, it was something. We would say the prayers and go through the regular Mass; he rarely gave much of a sermon.

There was no place to sit for Mass unless it was on the grass. If it was a dry day, that was fine. But if it was raining or when the snow came, you just stood in three or four rows, maybe 15 or 20 of us.

After I went down the hill a few times for Mass, some of the other guys asked about it. They wanted to go, but they didn't know what to do at a Catholic service.

"All you have to do is come," I assured them. "You can come down with me if you want to. It's not so much about being Catholic. It's about talking to God in prayer."

"What do I do after I get there?"

"Just do everything I do," I said. "If I kneel down, you kneel down. If I stand up, you stand up."

Well, they had no problem doing that. Some even continued to go to Mass the whole time we were in Korea.

Most, though, when we went back to Japan, never went again. I'd go to church, but they were not there. As soon as the immediate danger passed, they stopped going.

I used to think, *Gee, kind of fair weather friends*, you know. I think they really did believe in the back of their minds there is a God, but they didn't believe it strongly enough to get up off their tails and go to church on Sunday.

On the front, I prayed alone when I was on guard duty. I'd have half the night to be awake if there were just two of us in the hole. For four hours at a time, all you did was stand in your sleeping bag, keeping an eye out for the enemy. If it got really cold, I covered myself completely in the sleeping bag, except for my face and gloved hands. I had my rifle sticking out there for instant use if I needed it.

Amid that quiet, with all that time on my hands and with nothing to do but think, I would always take time to pray, maybe just say the "Our Father" and the "Hail Mary" and all the other prayers I knew, such as "The Act of Contrition." It would just be an extension of what prayers I would normally do at night.

During some brutal hours ahead, prayers would be my constant companion.

CHAPTER 8: Thanksgiving

A thick snow began falling one night when we were hunkered down in our trenches trying to keep warm. All was quiet. Suddenly, I heard a sharp *crack!* and then a *thump!* Then a whole area in front of our line lighted up. Something had triggered one of our trip flares.

A trip flare basically is a device with a long string. When someone trips over the string, it yanks a pin out and causes the flare to light up brightly. The idea was that, if the enemy was coming at us, he would trip that flare and light up the area around him for about five or ten minutes. During that time, we would be able to see him and shoot.

Crack! Thump! A second trip flare lit up.

Some of our guys started shooting and shooting and shooting. They were certain the enemy was racing toward us, triggering those flares.

This shooting went on for a little while until the captain saw that it was a one-sided battle – that, in fact, no one was shooting except us.

"Cease fire!" he yelled. "Cut it out, and reload your weapons!"

The firing petered out until, again, silence.

The captain figured out correctly that heavy snow was breaking tree branches, dropping them and tripping a couple of flares. The rest of the night, we continued to hear cracking in the distance and, occasionally, another flare would go off. But we never saw any enemy that night.

On the line, nerves always were on edge. Any little sound prompted some guys to fire up flare grenades, which lighted an area for more than a minute.

If there was an actual enemy attack, the Army shot up these big parachute flares high in the air, lighting up a whole hill as they slowly floated back to earth. The Army also had big searchlights they used if it was a cloudy night. The light reflected off the clouds, and it would almost seem like a moonlit night.

Smelly Socks

Bad weather added to the misery of being on the Jamestown Line. When it got really cold, the Army provided each of us with a parka as well as rubber boots with a wool-lined interior. They called these "shoe packs," which were supposed to help prevent us from getting frostbite and trench foot, but we still ended up with wet socks.

We all were assigned two pairs of socks at a time. Each morning, we had to take off our socks, stick the wet ones inside our shirts against our bellies, and put the other pair on. The heat from our bodies dried out the wet socks.

Of course, those socks got riper and riper as time went on. However after a while, we couldn't smell ourselves, so we didn't mind it, especially with all the other horrible odors from other things, living and dead.

After maybe two weeks, the Army brought each of us two new

pairs of socks, and we'd throw the old ones in a barrel and put the new ones on.

We got dirty very quickly on the front because we didn't have a chance to wash much. Once in a while we'd have a little bit of hot water to clean ourselves. The Army used some kind of immersible heater to boil water in these big 55-gallon drums. I would go there and get enough water in my steel helmet to shave. When I was done, I'd rinse it out, dry it a bit, and put the helmet back on my head.

We had enough water to shave, wash our faces and brush our teeth regularly, but we did not get a bath. Once, late in the fall, the Army did bring up portable showers. We went back of the line for a warm shower and some clean clothes.

To keep our head warm, we had a helmet liner. Underneath it, I wore a cap with a little bill on it. Our parka hoods had a fur lining, and the whole thing went right over the helmet and tied shut. I also had gloves to keep me warm.

We had loads of weapons to protect us along the Jamestown Line. In our trenches I saw grenades, bazookas and recoil-less rifles, which are pretty good-sized weapons; heavy machine-guns, .30-caliber and .50-caliber; all that stuff. I know there were flame-throwers up there, but I never saw one.

There were reports the Chinese had loud speakers they used to shout propaganda at Americans across the line, but I never heard that. I did hear bugles. When the enemy soldiers were going into battle, to build up their nerve, they'd blow bugles. If I heard that, I knew to get prepared for an attack. Once in a while, they blew the bugles just to rattle us, even if there was no one coming.

What About Fox Company?

We noticed in late November that — while we were being sent out to the outpost regularly — Fox Company wasn't part of the rotation, even though we were both part of the 2nd Battalion. We kept saying, "Well, what about Fox Company? They are just as close as we are to that outpost, but we're the ones taking care of it all the time."

Finally, our captain agreed. "Yeah. You know, that ain't right," he told us. So he got a hold of the colonel and said, "How about Fox Company? Why can't they share this outpost duty with George Company so we're not on it all the time?"

And the colonel said, "There's no reason they can't." So he ordered Fox Company to do the next few patrols to Hill 255.

Wednesday, November 21, the day before Thanksgiving, was the first time Fox Company was sent to outpost duty in quite a while. The captain told one or two squads of us from George Company that we had to go over across to Fox Company's position and fill in its part of the line, because it was short-handed there with its 3rd Platoon out on outpost duty.

As I recall it, we had our Thanksgiving meal a day early, maybe because part of Fox Company would be out at the outpost for the holiday. We were served turkey, potatoes, gravy, cranberries, rolls, peaches and vegetables, all thrown together. It tasted very good, and for once we could have all we wanted. Plastic bags were provided so we could take some leftovers back to the trench with us. We also got three cans of beer, several pieces of candy and some extra cigarettes.

I planned a lovely dining experience for the evening hours dug in with Fox Company on Thanksgiving Eve. But suddenly the enemy started shooting white phosphorus shells at our line. That usually means there was going to be an attack somewhere. It didn't have to be on our line. It could be deceptive. They could be shooting at us and attacking somewhere else.

The white phosphorus burned for hours. The enemy would shoot one of those shells to mark a certain spot on their map. Then they'd shoot another one and it marked a certain spot. Therefore, if they started shooting artillery, they should know where to aim it based on where that white phosphorus was burning.

The Outpost Is Under Attack

Just about dusk, it began to rain artillery shells. I mean, rain. They were everywhere. They were exploding. I swear to God there must have been 20,000 of them that went off in the next few hours.

Of course, I tried to keep my head down pretty well. But the officers came around and yelled, "Keep your head up and watching because they're liable to be coming at us. We don't know where they're going to attack."

The word soon came back that the Chinese were attacking the outpost with maybe thousands of troops going up against 48 of our men

It was chilling to know, had it not been for Fox Company taking over outpost duty from us, one of our platoons would have been there instead. I'm not sure whether it would have been my platoon or another group. It might have been us.

We did our best to help them. We were shooting down below the outpost. We had a tank that came up next to us and was aiming right down there, firing. The enemy shot everything but the kitchen sink at that tank. They were scared to death of that tank because the vehicle could really put the old stuffing into them.

The fighting continued from dark until after 2 o'clock in the morning, almost 3. All of a sudden, everything stopped. The enemy didn't shoot artillery anymore. They had taken the outpost.

At daylight, we learned the enemy had captured or killed every one of our guys on the outpost before abandoning it. I felt sick. I smoked a couple of cigarettes, but I didn't touch my bag of Thanksgiving leftovers or any of that beer.

Instead of breakfast, all my stomach could handle was a piece or two of Army candy.

Fox Company soon sent us back to our own outfit. We were walking down the hill, the whole bunch of us together, when we got right to the main path coming in from the outpost. There we saw a bunch of choggie boys carrying back the dead on cedar posts. They were all dead Americans, maybe 40 or so of them in a long line. Boy, that was not something you wanted to see every day.

To carry the dead, the choggie boys used wire to tie each soldier's hands together and his feet together. Then they lifted each one up like a big pig or something right on the cedar post. One Korean choggie boy on each end would carry out that soldier. That's 80 choggie boys in one long line. When they got to the ambulance, they slid a body off the post, took the wires off and put the body in the ambulance. Over and over, this process repeated.

There were 10 men or so from Fox Company the Army couldn't find alive or dead, including the lieutenant in charge, James L. Stone, so we knew they had been captured.

We Adapted Easily

We hadn't been back to our outfit for two hours when the officers ordered our platoon to go to the outpost. We didn't have to stay overnight, but we had to go out and check it over and everything.

All of the American dead had been picked up by then, but there were still 15 to 20 dead Chinese inside the barbed wire, just lying there. The rest outside the barbed wire had been picked up. The Army later estimated that 48 men from Fox Company had killed or wounded 1,500 of the enemy before the outpost was overrun.

It was really the first dead Chinese I had seen that close. One Chinese soldier had been hit in the stomach by a shell and his intestines were hanging out. But it was getting cool enough where the smell didn't bother me too much. It wasn't long before my appetite came back. I ate my lunch just 10 feet from dead enemy. It was another case of adapting easily when you're 19.

"There are booby traps here," the captain reminded us as we patrolled the outpost. "Don't touch anything, because it might explode on you." The next day, the Army sent the engineers out to get rid of all those booby traps and to rebuild the fences that were knocked down.

I kept this piece of Chinese propaganda lying on the ground after Fox Company was attacked on our outpost on Thanksgiving Eve 1951.

While at the outpost, I noticed a lot of papers scattered on the ground, and I pocketed some as souvenirs. They were little enemy leaflets, some of which had "Safe Conduct Pass" written on top from The Chinese People's Volunteers' Headquarters. The basic message was: "If you come over to our side and turn yourself in, you will be treated very well indeed." Truth was, we heard they abused their prisoners something awful. But to read that propaganda leaflet, you'd think they were going to treat us like kings, feed us steak every day.

We left the outpost by mid-afternoon on Thanksgiving. but it wasn't long before we were back up there again for more patrols. We didn't go so often, because Fox Company now had to go up there, too. Of course, they had a lot of new men to replace all those who were killed or captured.

As we entered December, the prospect of frostbite became a

real threat as temperatures plunged below freezing. I was not looking forward to several months of living outdoors during one of Korea's notoriously long, frigid winters.

CHAPTER 9: Christmas and New Year's Eve

In the Army, the enlisted soldiers tended to pass along any bit of "news," no matter where they heard it. George Company was no exception. We called them "shithouse rumors." We had no radio to tune in real news. Gossip and speculation, often dreadfully wrong, filled the vast void in what we were officially told.

The most common rumor was that peace talks were close to an agreement and that the war would soon be over and we would be going home. Another was that we would drop an atomic bomb and get the whole thing over that way.

Such stories typically would come and go. But about the beginning of December 1951, one rumor persisted.

"Did you hear? We're going home," one of my buddies told me.

And I said, "What the hell are you talking about?"

He said, "We're going to be replaced by another outfit, the 45th (Infantry Division), and we're leaving for Japan."

"You dumb bunny," I said. "You're making it twice as hard on yourself. We're not going back to Japan. It's another rumor. How many times have you been fooled?"

"No, no, LaRue. I heard this from somebody who knows,"

another guy piped in.

"For shit's sake," I said, "don't spread that crap around. We're not going anywhere."

Most nodded and agreed it was probably nothing.

Then on December 13, the captain called us down to the foot of the hill.

"Well, I got good news for you guys. We're going back to Japan. We're being replaced by the 45th."

Some of the guys immediately laughed and pointed at me. "See, LaRue! You didn't know what the hell you were talking about!"

I was so happy that I didn't care whether I was right or wrong. The 1st Cavalry Division was due for a rest, but the last thing I expected was being pulled off the line after just three months in Korea. In fact, we were informed that anyone with less than two months would stay with the new division. Everyone immediately began counting their time on the line. Only a few unfortunate men had to stay with the 45th.

Teasing the Poor Bastards

Soon, officers of the 45th arrived. We had to show them the lines of fire, where the enemy was, and generally try to help a green division adjust to being on the line.

The next day after that, December 16, the captain told us to grab our stuff and sit on the backside of the hill as we waited for the troops from the 45th to arrive. For a little while, nobody was watching for the enemy. Had the Chinese known we weren't looking, they probably would have attacked right then and been very successful.

It wasn't long before we saw this whole line of 45th Division guys with shiny helmets and clean uniforms coming right by us up the hill. And, of course, we were the old combat veterans and so we had to give them a little lip.

We shouted, "Hey, look at this! Boy, those uniforms look really clean!" And so on. We were giving them a hard time. Of course, the poor bastards didn't want to be there any more than we did.

Apparently, they had instructions they weren't to respond if we said anything. All they did was walk by gloomily and say, "Hi, fellas," and just went where they were supposed to be.

As soon as they were settled in, our captain told us to move out. We left on the same trucks that brought in the guys from the 45th.

We were taken about 10 miles behind the line, where we moved into big tents with kerosene heaters at each end. It was still a little chilly in there because the tents weren't insulated, but it seemed heavenly compared with the trenches.

That's when we learned that both the 5th Cavalry and 7th Cavalry had already been there and then shipped out to Japan. Our 8th Cavalry was the last of the three regiments of the 1st Cavalry Division to come off the line.

Even then, they held us back from leaving Korea completely until the Army was sure the 45th Infantry Division could hold the line. In fact, the Chinese did immediately attack them. We could hear the sound of fighting around the clock for a few days, and we worried that we might be ordered back to the line to support them. However, the 45th held, much to our relief.

During the two weeks back in that staging area, the guys had a grand old time. We partied, we sang, we ate and we watched movies. I still remember how wonderful it was to see Gene Kelly in "Singin' in the Rain." We also spent the evenings talking about what we were going to do when we got back to civilization.

It got extremely cold in those two weeks, and despite those two red-hot space heaters in every tent, we could only stay warm by climbing into our sleeping bags.

A Special Christmas Mass

On Christmas Eve, those of us who wanted to go to Mass got aboard a truck and rode to a huge tent set up in a field. It was the biggest tent I had ever seen in my life, but by the time we got there, there was no room for a single person more to squeeze inside.

We had to stand kind of halfway in the door and halfway out, trying to see and hear the service. It was close to zero degrees under clear skies. But it was pretty nice inside the tent because of hundreds and hundreds of men packed in there. It was a little like standing at the door of a barn warmed with body heat of cattle. Since we were partly outside, we also stomped a bit and moved around to shake off the chill.

After the Mass, we were all given coffee and doughnuts. It

was my best Christmas ever, and that comes from someone who has enjoyed many good ones. It truly was a magical moment to be standing there, the sky clear as a bell with all the stars. It seemed the brightest might be the Star of Bethlehem. I remember thinking that it was almost like that first Christmas. The Lord had brought us through our trial, we had traveled a long way and now we had a place where we were safe.

Shortly after our regiment arrived, black market British beer, or ale, suddenly appeared, and we were able to buy a case for $2. Some guys celebrated by getting pretty well snookered on the cheap beer. I had a few, too, but then got into my bag and went to sleep, my unloaded M1 rifle tucked beside me with my duffel bag.

Some of the others in a corner of our tent partied all night when we first got beer, including one short, blonde-haired PFC who got really drunk. He got all wound up in the moment and pulled out his pistol, swinging it around.

Suddenly: *Bang! Bang!*

That blast of gunfire made every awake in the tent. As I sat up, I noticed a bullet lying next to my head, with a brand new hole in my sleeping bag. I jumped to my feet.

"Holy shit, somebody shot at me!" I yelled, holding up the bullet.

Some others started hollering. People began pointing and yelling at this blonde PFC, who was literally holding the smoking gun.

"Hey, what the hell are you doing? You pretty near shot somebody," someone said.

And, boy, everything got quiet over there all of a sudden. That was the end of their party for the night. The PFC didn't say a word more, and nobody reported him. I know I wasn't going to be the guy to report a soldier who had just been in combat.

The Joy of Warm Air

The day before New Year's Eve, the Army put all of us from the 8th Cavalry aboard trucks and drove us to a railroad station to board a troop train. It was freezing inside the train cars. There was no heat at all, and the seats were hard planks. We were told we would be traveling all night and would be taken off in the morning. We weren't told exactly where we were going next.

Two or three guys pulled out their bedding to keep warm and to have a little cushion while they slept. When one of the sergeants saw that, he warned us that anyone who didn't have his bedding stowed when we got off the train, the Army would send him back to the front. I knew that was bull, of course, but I for one did not want to risk going back up there. So I just spent the night shivering, trying to get some sleep, while the guys who did grab bedding were deep in slumber.

Just about daybreak, we discovered we were in Inchon, the same port on the western side of Korea where, months before, Gen. MacArthur turned around the war with a brilliantly executed invasion.

After the train stopped, we had to get everything together quickly. And, of course, those guys with bedding had it folded and back in place and were ready to leave with the rest of us.

Inchon was an extremely shallow port and only useable when the tide came in. We sat on the beach most of the day awaiting the high tide. As soon as it came in late in the afternoon, the landing craft came in for us. We were loaded aboard and taken out about a mile or so to some Navy troop transports. To get us aboard, the craft docked at this concrete pier. We then went up steps to a platform then took us across a gangplank onto the ship, all the while carrying our gear.

I photographed this last glimpse of Korea from the ship that transported us to Japan.

When we got aboard that ship, many of us noticed these big ventilators spewing bad air out of the ship. If the air from them smelled, we didn't notice. All we could think about was that wonderful heat. We just stood there and soaked it up.

Soon we were ordered into the bowels of the ship, with its beautiful sweet-smelling warmth. They assigned George Company to its own hold where we would sleep on these canvas bunks – four or five on top of each other, just a few inches apart. I grabbed a bottom one and put my bag on it.

Keep in mind I had not showered or bathed in weeks. I badly needed a haircut. Like most others, I hadn't shaved in a long time, either. We stunk. Our clothes stunk. We had been cold and filthy dirty for weeks.

"You're going to take a shower and you're going to wash your hair and get yourself clean," an officer told us. "So take all your clothes off and throw them in that drum next to the shower. Any personal stuff you've got, just lock up in your duffel bag before you go in there. And when you come out, we'll have clean clothes for you."

So I stripped right down to nothing and went in and showered. Because I hadn't had a haircut in three months, my hair was long and curly with big ringlets, the longest it had been in my life.

I had cracks in the palms of my hands that bled because they were chapped so badly. They were just open sores. When I showered, I got all the dirt and dried blood and everything cleaned out.

They had clothes waiting for us, including uniform, socks, shoes and underclothes. Our old clothing was put in trash cans and probably thrown overboard.

It wasn't long after that, over the loudspeaker, we heard it was chow time. They sent our whole company up together to the mess hall. I hadn't had a meal indoors for months and months, except for inside a tent. And this was a Navy ship with Navy chow, which is always very good.

Happy New Year

I was given my first civilized dinner since I left Pusan. I was sitting down at a table like a human being, not on the ground or squeezed into a trench. The Navy outdid itself, and the food was like manna from heaven. I'm sure it was one of the best-tasting meals I ever had, simply because I hadn't had a decent meal in such a long time. We were even allowed seconds. We were a tough, battle-hardened group, lean and healthy as one could get, and we ate until it seemed we could hold no more, and then ate again.

After we stuffed ourselves, we went back to our bunks. We all just wanted to sleep again because we were finally warm and our stomachs were full. Those of us on a lower bunk just had to remember to sleep right in the center in case somebody above got sick and threw up. I never got sick and, fortunately that night, neither did anyone else above me.

Soon we were all asleep, and someone put the lights out. At midnight, this loudspeaker came on and said, "Now hear this. Now hear this. It's midnight. Happy New Year, everybody."

And everybody cheered. We had survived to see 1952. Then we rolled over and went back to sleep.

The next morning, we enjoyed breakfast with almost the same vigor as we ate dinner. Then we were kind of free to roam, so we went up on deck to look. We were way out in the Yellow

Sea. We could see the Korean shoreline, with rather pointed rocks protruding from the sea, like large sentinels. In the early morning sun, it was a beautiful sight.

Even more stirring was the vast array of transports, destroyers, battleships and carriers traveling with us. I had thought ours was the only ship, but we were in a small armada necessary to transport the whole 8th Cavalry.

We watched as sailors passed things back and forth over cables from ship to ship. Planes occasionally flew over our fleet. I spent as much time as I could on deck watching all the activity. We had nothing else to do except eat our meals and tend to our personal hygiene.

Late in the evening on January 2, we arrived in the port of Hakodate, on the northern island of Hokkaido, Japan. The ship was soon unloaded and we were put aboard a train heading north. As we rode the train, which was heated, it was dark outside and that only added to my wonderment as we passed little lighted villages where you could see many thatched roof huts and people walking around in traditional Japanese clothing.

We rode all night, but most of us weren't sleeping. We just smiled and talked and visited. Some time at night, around 2 in the morning, the train stopped, and they put us in Army trucks and took us to an Army base known as Camp Chitose II. The base was just outside the Japanese town of Chitose and about 30 miles east of Sapporo.

After settling into Quonset hut barracks and getting a good night's sleep, our first order of business was to have the biggest party of our lives.

CHAPTER 10: Beer and Candy

Usually, beer in the barracks is an absolute no-no everywhere in the Army. It's a punishable offense to bring it in. But for two weeks after we arrived at Camp Chitose II, we were authorized to have beer in our barracks. It was our reward for serving in combat.

The Army opened a warehouse and sold us beer – I think it was Schlitz – for $1 for a 24-can case. We were allowed a maximum of two cases each. So, for just two bucks, I had all the beer I could drink. What I didn't have in my hand I stored in my locker.

The partying at George Company was something to see. We proceeded to have the biggest, happiest drunk of all time. And there was no marching, no training, no nothing. The only real restriction was that we couldn't go off-base into the nearby Japanese town of Chitose for those two weeks. But we didn't mind. We were so happy to be out of Korea. Even guys who didn't like each other put aside animosities for those two weeks. We just got back from some of the worst conditions possible. We were all buddies then. I'm sure the rest of the soldiers in the 1st Cavalry Division were having similar parties in their own barracks.

Our barracks soon stunk of beer. Guys tossed their empty cans just about anywhere. We went to bed when we wanted, we got up when we wanted, we partied when we wanted.

Then suddenly it all ended.

On January 16, the captain came into the barracks early in the morning.

"As of today, the fun's over," he said. "As of today, there's no more drinking in the barracks. I want all the beer, including all the empty beer cans, picked up and removed from the barracks."

He pointed to a spot in the yard where the Army wanted us to put every beer can. Within an hour, a 20-foot-high hill of cans sprouted in that spot. Most were empties. Unless you had been there, you wouldn't have believed fewer than 200 guys could have consumed that much beer in two weeks.

If we had any beer left, we still had to put it that pile. Trucks soon came around and hauled it all away. (I always wondered if someone ended up salvaging all that free beer still in unopened cans and cases.)

We then had to take out all the bunk beds to thoroughly scrub down the barracks. When we finished cleaning, there wasn't a scent of beer anywhere. By the time we brought the bunks back in and straightened up the barracks, you never would have known we just been partying for two weeks.

It was back to the good old Army we knew and hated: marches and training, often led now by newcomers who knew less about combat than most of us.

The mission of 1st Cavalry Division was no longer to defend hills along the Jamestown Line. We transitioned very quickly from that very hot war in Korea to the Cold War against the

Soviet Union. Our base was located on Hokkaido, which is separated in northern Japan by just a few miles of water from the Soviet island of Sakhalin. We knew the Russians, if they decided to invade Japan, likely would have started at Hokkaido. So American troops were stationed there not only as a deterrent but also to spy on Russian broadcasts and to monitor their military traffic in the region.

Of course, as with all things in the military, the mission of the 1st Cavalry Division could change at any time, and it did later. It was always possible the Army would send us right back into fighting.

But as I got ready to turn 20 on January 27, I had little understanding of the mission of the 1st Cavalry. My biggest concerns at the moment were mostly personal.

I was due a promotion to corporal from my current rank as a PFC. I had my time in, plus I had served in combat. But suddenly the powers-that-be decided to freeze all rank overseas for one year. The reason given was that battlefield promotions had created too many corporals and sergeants, and the number had to drop before more promotions could be made. That, of course, was bullshit. We all knew it was a cost-savings measure because rank was not frozen in the States. This freezing of rank resulted in men coming overseas and outranking some of us who had more time and combat experience. It was another example of the basic unfairness of the military.

90-Day Wonders

When we first arrived at Chitose II, most of our officers acted extraordinarily nice to us. They had served with us in combat.

We were very close to them. Being human, it was hard for these officers to be disciplinarians with us. How could you yell at an enlisted guy who might have saved your life in the battlefield? The Army knew that, which is why one of the first things it did was transfer most of our officers back to the States.

In their place came a bunch of what are widely known as "90-day wonders." These were officers who had only been in the service maybe six months. They had trained in Officer Candidate School, but they weren't experienced like us in combat or even in many other ways of Army life.

We had one of these new officers teaching a class in combat tactics. Some of the stuff, which these officers had learned in school, we knew to be absolutely stupid in real combat. One day, one of these officers told us something that didn't make sense, and a few of the guys started to giggle.

"Did I say something wrong?" the officer asked.

"Sir, that isn't the way we did it in Korea." And the soldier would proceed to explain how that tactic could get a lot of our people killed needlessly. Of course, that would embarrass the shit out of the officer. This kept happening repeatedly.

Finally, several officers complained to our captain. The captain was one of the few officers still around who had served with us in Korea, so all the guys respected him. He came marching into our classroom and stood there, and he began talking to us in a mocking tone.

"I know all your big combat veterans feel you know more than these guys do. But their job is to teach you," the captain said.

"And the next man who laughs or says something when these men are trying to teach you, you are going to get court-martialed."

Well, that was the end of fun. We started settling down and taking orders, and there was no more baloney on our part.

'10,000 Whores'

Not long after we got rid of beer in the barracks, the entire 2nd Battalion of the 8th Cavalry Regiment was called outside in the middle of winter to the parade field. As we shivered, we got a lecture in personal conduct from Lt. Col. Robert E. Wallace.

He told us we now had permission to go into the town of Chitose, just outside the gates of our base. He warned us to avoid getting into any kind of conflict with the Japanese. It had only been seven years since we dropped the atom bombs on Japan to end World War II. Japan was still under American occupation in January 1952, although the United States was about to formally hand back governance. The Army warned us we might run into a hot-head or Communist agitator happy to pick a fight over our continued presence. Wallace didn't need some American G.I. involved in an international incident.

Wallace seemed equally concerned about our relationships with Japanese women.

"Gentlemen, there's something like 10,000 whores in this town," Wallace said, drawing out the word "whores" is a booming voice. "Some of them got VD. So I would advise you guys to stay away from them. If you want to go into town, that's fine. There are bars to go into. You can buy stuff. But stay away from the whores."

Well, our guys couldn't wait to get to town to get to the whores.

On payday, especially if it fell on a Saturday, everyone on the base headed for town. Chitose must have had 300 taverns, along with shops that sold trinkets and gaudy clothing that soldiers sent home to their loved ones. The place was a magnet for young, sexually active soldiers.

Japanese people were known for being very clean, cleaner than we are, but most didn't have running water in their homes. So when you walked downtown at night, you could walk right by these buildings with people showering inside – men and women. You could see them right through a great big plate-glass window on the front, kind of fogged up a little bit, but there were hundreds and hundreds of naked bodies in there and they were all showering at the same time.

The favorite thing for the guys to do was to walk by very slowly and take a good look. And at 19, 20 years old, you did. You learned a lot. But the Japanese were very blasé about it. They weren't looking at anybody else; they were just kind of staring off at the ceiling and showering. When they got through, they got dressed and they left.

As Col. Wallace had so indelicately pointed out, Chitose had thousands of prostitutes. Mostly dressed in Western style clothing, these women lined the streets, shouting to the guys, encouraging them to sample their wares. Many of those girls were quite attractive and, after a guy had a few beers, they all seemed lovely. Some of the prostitutes didn't come out on the street, staying in a window somewhere, waving at you to get you to come in.

The U.S. Army Military Police were very visible in the town, checking for problems with the GIs. The Japanese police only handled their own people who got out of hand. The Japanese were especially tough on the prostitutes. Prostitution was legal, but every girl had to go once a week and be inspected by a medical team. Each prostitute was supposed to carry what we called a "bingo card." Every week, she got a stamp on that card saying she was free of venereal diseases. Every GI had the right to walk up to a girl soliciting prostitution on the street and say, "I want to see your bingo card."

The Japanese cops would patrol, and, boy, those girls better not be on the street if they were dirty. You could always tell if there was someone on the street who wasn't supposed to be there because, when the Japanese police came around the corner in a jeep, these girls would run like hell and disappear into the houses. They would stay indoors, but they would try to get you to come in.

Most of the guys who fooled around with any of the prostitutes always picked one on the street, not one in a house. If they were in a house, that's probably because they were infected. Of course, some guys were dumber than a box of rocks. If they saw a girl and liked the looks of her – and some of them were awfully pretty – well, they didn't give a damn. They'd go in and take their chance. More than one of them ended up with VD.

It was such a problem that each barracks had a front cadre room purposely for guys to go and get treatment for VD. I happened to sleep near that room. At night, I'd see a guy pad down there, shut the door, and the next thing I knew I would hear a slap on the rear then a little, "Oooh!" And you knew a guy just got a shot. I think it took two or three shots of penicillin to cure the VD. The reason they did this at night is because treatments were all very unofficial. The Army did it this way to keep VD treatments off a guy's military record.

The Bar Girls

My buddies and I stuck with visiting the bars, meeting the girls who worked there. Our initial favorite was The White Bear. It even had a picture of a bear on the front of it. Like all of the taverns, The White Bear was set up with one girl for each table. She would serve us, then sit at our table as long as we stayed. The bar mostly served Japanese rice beer, which I thought was better than American beer.

These waitresses were just that – waitresses. They were usually more attractive than the street girls, so guys went back time and again just to keep meeting them. These bar girls weren't whores, but they had a different attitude about sex than most American girls had then. I mean, if the bar girl liked you, it was okay to have sex – and it was free.

Right away after we started to visit the bar, the Japanese girls wanted to know our first names. We all gave them our nicknames, or they made some up for us, which we started using. My best friend was Don Davis, but the Japanese girls called him Chibi, which is Japanese for "small person."

The guys introduced me as Kenny, but when the girls said it, they pronounced my name as "Candy." The guys thought that was funny, so from then on they called me Candy, too, even when they wrote letters after I was out of the service. It wasn't the most flattering of nicknames, but almost everyone in the service had one. My buddies had nicknames like Moose and

Tex and Tall and Chic and, of course, Chibi.

From left to right, Don Davis, me, John Bello and O.B. Smith enjoy a few beers at the Lucky-1 tavern in Chitose in 1952.

We had one Army buddy from New York State who was always bragging about his sexual exploits with women, especially with a girlfriend back home. He had a photo of her on the inside of his wallet. Over and over, he would show us her picture and say things like, "Look at that. I had her. I shagged her," and all that business.

We all suspected he was a virgin.

One of the other guys was seeing this prostitute in Chitose. Her Americanized name was Jackie, and she looked like a movie star. She was one of the prettiest girls I had seen over there. One night, she agreed to test our theory about our buddy.

We got to a table in a bar downtown and she immediately attached herself to this New York guy. And she would say things like "Come on with me," and she pulled at him seductively. It didn't take too much persuasion for him to go off into a room with her because she was so attractive.

About 10 minutes later, she starts yelling, "Cherry boy! Cherry boy! Cherry boy!" That was the slang term Japanese prostitutes used for a GI who was a virgin. Of course, we thought it was absolutely the funniest thing. Our buddy soon came out of there, his face as red as a cherry. He never again bragged to us about all the women he had.

Later we found a place called the No. 2 Beer Hall, which was huge. It had a big main room, maybe 150 feet long and probably 75 feet wide, with a lower floor and a 10-foot balcony that went all the way around the second floor. We sat in the upper part and looked down at whatever was going on. They had some really risqué floor shows there, much more than anything you'd see in the United States at the time.

A Japanese Girlfriend

In Chitose, if a soldier met a bar girl that he really liked, he could arrange to set up housekeeping. He would pay 30 dollars American a month, and the girl would find an apartment and move in with her stuff. She was then the exclusive girlfriend of her American soldier. Ordinarily, the two lived almost like husband and wife, and when he was off-duty, they lived together, going to the movies or spending a quiet evening.

I had a girlfriend like that for several months. I've since forgotten her name, it's been so long. At the time I thought the relationship was good for her and good for me. Thirty dollars was a lot of money then. She didn't have to do a heck of a lot, and she was paid handsomely. It wasn't like these girls were forced to get into these relationships. If a girl didn't like the guy, she wouldn't do it. At the time, I didn't think our relationship was that serious. I don't believe she ever assumed she would come with me once I left Japan.

It was rare for any of the soldiers to marry these girls, but some guys did fall in love. It was very tough for these men to ship home, leaving these women that they had spent so many months seeing. A few didn't leave them behind. They married the girls and brought them stateside.

On the other hand, I remember one guy we thought might marry this girl because they were so close. But when it came time to go home, he dropped her like a hot potato and left. She was devastated, to say the least.

Of course, the result of all this sex among Japanese women and GIs is that many illegitimate children were born. These babies were often shunned by Japanese and put into orphanages. To me, that is the tragic part of this story.

CHAPTER 11: The Hokkaido Bear

Not long after I returned to Japan, I sent Dad some photos of Chinese war dead that I photographed just after Fox Company was overrun at the outpost. I took them mainly to prove to my father I was there. Dad couldn't wait to run to the Courier and Freeman newspaper in Potsdam to show the editor the photos. Of course, the paper couldn't print anything like that.

That's me, front and center, showing an unsteady mastery of skiing during winter training in Japan in early 1952.

However, a few days later the newspaper published a brief story quoting my letter in which I told my parents I enjoyed a full day of skiing near the base in Hokkaido. "I took a lot of spills," I said, "and am I sore today!"

Just in case someone thought I might be having too much of a good time, the editor added: "Private LaRue is with a group that has been withdrawn from the front lines in Korea and is now training for winter fighting in skiing, snowshoeing and other arts necessary to be effective in the snow."

The article continued, "He was trained first as a radar technician, but when he was sent to Korea, he was transferred to the First Cavalry Division and sent to the front. For two or three months he was in the thick of fighting. He has sent home to his parents pictures he took Thanksgiving Day, after an evening attack by the Chinese the day before. The ground was strewn with dead bodies, mostly of the enemy."

My former platoon leader Newton "Steve" Babcock huddles near a warming can during ski training around February 1952.

Winter training was fun. We did cross-country skiing. We also learned how to move fast on snowshoes in woods and fields and everywhere. We also would do military exercises where we set up a perimeter defense, and we'd dig in. But instead of shooting at each other, we'd have snowball fights. That was a lot of fun, too.

We did ski training until the snow melted in the spring, then we switched over around April to summer training with 20-mile marches carrying a heavy pack.

After one of those marches, my back began to ache. It hurt like hell and was swollen by 6 inches or so. I marched on, hoping that it was temporary, but I soon had to go to sick call. Some medic looked me over, strapped me up with some kind of cloth, and sent me right back to duty. My back swelled up all over again, and the medics sent me right back with a tighter wrap.

By chance, right after one of those marches, the Army held what is known euphemistically as a "short-arm inspection." That's where the doctors come by at 5 o'clock in the morning to examine everyone's "short arm" for venereal disease. We jumped out of bed and stood at attention while doctors checked to see whether we had a drip or not. They did this in the morning so guys with VD wouldn't have a chance to hide it.

As I stood waiting, a lieutenant asked me about that swelling in my back and the strap around it.

"Sir, every time I go on a long field exercise and I'm carrying too much weight, my back swells."

"Well, why don't you go to sick call?"

"I did so, sir. Twice. And all they did was strap me up and send me back."

"Well, they won't anymore," the lieutenant said. "I want you to go right to the medics first thing this morning. I'll explain to them that they're not to do that again, that they're to arrange to find out what's wrong with you."

"Yes, sir."

Back Surgery or Not?

The medics this time sent me to Sapporo Army Hospital for an exam and X-rays. After that, I got called into an office where a doctor studied my medical records a bit before looking up at me.

"You have what is called spondylitis, which basically is a displaced back bone in your spine. It's a congenital condition. You were born with it," he said. "You wouldn't even notice it probably unless you put too much weight on it."

He gave me two choices: I could have back surgery or he could ask the Army to put me on a softer job.

The thought of Army doctors digging around my spine sent a chill right up it.

"Sir, I'd prefer not to have the back operation if I can avoid it. I've never had problems as long as I didn't have to stress my back like that," I said.

"What do you want to do?"

"I was trained in radar repair but got called up to combat. I would like to go back to radar if I could," I said.

He smiled. "We'll see what we can do."

Sure enough, in a couple of days, I got orders to transfer over to the 1st Cavalry Division's Artillery Headquarters – the same unit I originally had been sent to in Korea to do radar repair. Artillery headquarters was at Chitose I, just a few miles away.

It was hard saying goodbye to my buddies in George Company; we had been through a lot together. But I was glad I wouldn't have to go on any more long marches.

At Artillery Headquarters, my first stop was to see a captain whom I hoped would arrange my transfer to radar repair. When I walked into his office, I'm sure my mouth dropped open. It was Captain Patrick J. Troy, the same officer who had sent me to the front the previous October.

He seemed delighted to see me.

"You know, I really have always wondered whatever happened to you guys. I had to ship you up to the front. I didn't like it, but I had to do it," he said.

Captain Troy's voice grew quieter. "Was it rough up there?"

I nodded. "Yes. Sometimes."

"I'm very glad to see you survived it."

He picked up my paperwork, which noted my request for duty

that wasn't so physically demanding.

"What would you like to do?"

"Well, sir, the reason I transferred back here is because I am a trained radar repairman and I want to repair radars."

Captain Troy kind of chuckled.

"All our radars are in Korea," he told me, pausing to let it sink in that I would have to return to a war zone if I wanted that job. I told him that, in that case, I wouldn't be interested in radar repair.

He noted there was an opening for a clerk-typist where he worked in S3 Operations, which was the unit that planned the strategy of war and actually led troops that carried it out. That kind of office job sounded good to me. (I didn't tell him I barely passed typing in high school.)

At S3, I learned quickly. I did all the typing for an office initially consisting of one colonel, one major, two captains, one general's orderly and a master sergeant, whose main responsibility was to supervise me. Fortunately, the sergeant knew nothing of office work. As long as I satisfied the officers, he let me do pretty much as I wanted.

Col. Leon Bieri and Me

Col. Leon Bieri, a West Point man whose brusque manner left many shaken, headed our office. He was a chubby, pear-shaped man who didn't look like he was physically in shape to actually command men in combat. Some of the other soldiers behind his back called him the Hokkaido Bear. I didn't because I was afraid I might slip and say it in front of him sometime.

I stand outside my Chitose I barracks, which one of the guys decorated with non-regulation flower boxes. The Army didn't usually let you do things like that, but they let us in this case.

The first time I went into Col. Bieri's office to give him something to sign, he looked at me and got a sour look on his face.

"LaRue," he barked, "can't you straighten up your uniform? It looks kind of sloppy."

I'm sure my uniform was a little wrinkled, or maybe I didn't have it tucked in properly. I really worked hard to fix it, but he still would complain about my uniform practically every time I walked into his office. Finally, he gave up, because he knew I was trying, even if I wasn't doing the best work at it.

As time went on, Col. Bieri became more and more attached to me for some reason. The first thing I knew, he treated me almost like he was my father.

One day when I went into his office, he looked up and said very kindly, "So, private, tell me where you're from?"

He started asking me questions, like, "What did you do before you got into the service?" and "What do you plan to do when you got out?" He seemed genuinely interested in my answers. I just had to make sure pretty much every sentence out of my mouth included a "yes, sir" or "no, colonel" or whatever.

Funny thing, Col. Bieri didn't stop criticizing others about their appearance. He would regularly jump all over corporals or sergeants or even lieutenants.

"You look kind of sloppy today," he said one day to a chaplain.

The chaplain just nodded, "Yes, sir," but I could see him glance over at me with a slight expression that seemed to say, "Look at him, and you're worried about me?" But the chaplain never dared say anything to me, because I worked with Col. Bieri.

Close Call at the Supply Room

I did my best, though, to keep my uniform's appearance looking crisp. Every couple of months, I visited the supply room for fresh clothing. It was all professionally cleaned, but always second-hand.

One day there was a guy ahead of me in line turning in a .45-caliber pistol. The sergeant signed it in and everything, and the guy left. Just as I was walking to the counter, the sergeant took the gun and racked it a couple of times, pointed it right beside me on the counter and pulled the trigger. *Bang!* The bullet drove a hole right through the top of the counter next to my arm, came out the front, hit the floor and went sideways into the room next door. It made three holes.

Let me tell you that was one surprised supply sergeant and that was one surprised me. Once again, I was nearly shot by a U.S. soldier's careless handling of a firearm. The sergeant apologized and quickly gave me some replacement clothes, and I went back to the barracks.

A while later, a corporal told me to report immediately to a captain. When I got there, he said, "I understand something happened back here in the supply room."

"Yes, sir."

"Do you know you have the right to press charges against him for that, if you desire to."

I said, "Sir, I don't want to get anybody in trouble. As far as I'm concerned, it never happened."

"Good. In that case, we'll patch all three holes, nobody will ever know the difference and that will be the end of it. Just don't talk about it to anybody."

"OK, sir."

I went back and all but forgot all about it. Two months later, I had to go again to the supply room and get fresh clothes. I handed my old ones to this same sergeant who had accidentally fired the gun. He came out with everything brand new. I never got brand new Army clothes before. It was always used.

"Geez, thank you," I said, delighted at the especially crisp clothing. It wasn't until I got back to the barracks that I realized: *Wow, that son of a gun gave me new stuff because I didn't bring charges against him.* Indeed, every time afterward, whenever I visited the supply room, I got brand new clothing.

Smuggling Cigarettes

For a long while working for Col Bieri, I was still a PFC. Finally, in October 1952, word came that a bunch of us who had served in Korea would become "acting corporals." We didn't get the higher pay, but we had the rights to go to the service club and to give orders to PFCs or privates if the Army needed a corporal in charge of something. For us, here was the proof that the Army didn't freeze rank because there were too many corporals in the Far East. They just didn't want to give us raises.

In January 1953, I was finally promoted to corporal with full pay. That gave me $140 a month, including extra for being in combat. Of that, I put $50 into savings that went home to my mother, and she put it in the bank. When I got out of the service I had $1,700 in that savings account, which in those days, when people were paid $1 an hour, was a good bit of money.

Japan was a very inexpensive place to live, particularly if you were a soldier. The Army fed us. The Army clothed us. But at the end of the month, I often needed a little extra beer money.

One trick I learned was to go into the PX and buy two cartons of Camel or Lucky Strike cigarettes at $1 a carton. I took out the cigarettes, flattened the cartons, put them inside my shirt, put the cigarettes all the way around them, put on my heavy winter coat and went out through the gate. When I got to town, there was a place that bought cartons of American cigarettes for $4 each. I reassembled the two cartoons, sold them and made six bucks. That was enough to buy beer until payday.

Back at S3, I was given more and more responsibilities as time went on. I was assigned to the Hokkaido Air Alert switchboard, connecting our office with all the various commands on the island. If Russia decided to invade, we would know it first, and I was in charge of alerting others from our early-warning outpost. The Russians never attacked, but I got to handle a lot of alerts during practice drills.

Because that switchboard had to be maintained at all times, I was allowed to stay in the office when everyone else from the base had to go in the field on maneuvers. Only once did I go out, and that was as an assistant umpire during war games, telling the officers which of them had won the various battles and who was considered dead and out of the game. More than one officer became furious at me when he was told he was "dead." But the officers were instructed to bite their lips and take orders from a mere corporal because I worked with Col. Bieri.

I did have to pull guard duty on a regular basis. It wasn't hard work, but it was at night and it was cold sometimes. In winter, I had to stand outside this locked shack at the entrance to the motor pool.

Everyone on that duty was supposed to stay outside. However, some soldier figured out that, if you fooled around with the window, it would open a bit and we could climb inside the shack where it was warm. If we heard the corporal of the guard coming, we would just open the window and jump back outside. Most of the time the corporal of the guard was a friend of mine and wasn't going to do anything, even if he caught me inside.

Our office building was right next to an old Japanese air base, and you could see both military and commercial jets taking off and landing. One day, I heard sirens and looked out the front window. There was smoke coming up at the end of the runway. One of the jets didn't make it during takeoff, and it crashed right into the woods.

Secret Mission in Korea

In fall of 1952, I was granted "secret" clearance for classified information. The Army first had intelligence officers come to my mother and father's house in Norwood. They even talked to my teachers to make sure I was trustworthy. The reason for the secrecy: The Army was planning a mock invasion of Korea, called "Operation Feint," and they had a planning room set up right next to our main office, with a guard on the door and me typing up all this classified material. As soon as I got done, the captain would come in, pick it all up, check it over and then arrange for its distribution.

The idea of "Operation Feint" was to fool the enemy into thinking we were launching a surprise attack. We were going to bring in thousands and thousands of troops right up near Inchon. The goal was to get the enemy out on the roads to stop what they thought was an invasion. Then we would fire upon and bomb them and take out as many as we could before turning around the ships and going back to Japan without our soldiers ever coming ashore. Besides inflicting casualties, we wanted to test how quickly the Chinese would come out and defend the coast.

It turned out, according to what I've read since, that the operation wasn't very successful. The enemy launched a few shells but didn't mobilize heavily against the "invading" troops. Either they were incapable of defending such an invasion or they weren't really fooled at all.

Back at S3, we eventually moved to a bigger office in the front of the building, which had been a Japanese naval training center during World War II. Col. Bieri was in one corner and another colonel next to him. In the next room, just beyond the general's orderly, was an office with Brigadier General Ralph C. Cooper.

Every time General Cooper came into the office, I was on my feet right away with a salute. One day, he came up to me and said, "Corporal, it's not necessary to jump up every time I come in. Yes, if I come in with another general officer, you better be right on your feet. But you don't need to do that if it's just me." From then on, every time he strolled in the door, I looked to see if there was another general with him. Only once did that ever happen, and that was with the corps commander, Creighton Abrams. Boy, did I jump to attention. He was a big shot and very well known all over the country.

Our office also had two captains. One was Patrick Troy, who was the nicest of the bunch, and another I didn't like very well. He was always upset at me because he didn't think I was doing his typing and other paperwork fast enough. The problem was that I had orders to do the work by rank, not who gave it to me first. So this captain's paperwork got done only if I didn't have anything pending from the general or colonel.

At the end of big office was a 7-foot-high wall safe with a big steel door. One day Col. Bieri explained to me that, during World War II, the Japanese kept a picture of the emperor and a lock of his hair in there. When a class was ready to graduate from the naval academy, the Japanese brought the sailors into the room. They knelt down and put their heads on the floor in front of this display. The Japanese would have this big ceremony before closing the safe and locking it. Now with U.S. occupation, I had the combination to unlock the safe and access to its contents. I used it to keep our paper supplies.

While working in S3, I got around to tracking down radar school buddy Amel E. Landgraf, who had sailed on the Meigs with me. He wrote back in June 1952 to say he was now stationed in Japan repairing radars at a camp near Tokyo.

"Hiya, Ken. Man, was it good to hear from you," Landgraf wrote. "I hadn't known that you all had been in Korea. But I figured you probably went there because six of the seven of us (sent to the Far East from radar school) went there. The rest of us had it much easier than you did."

Of the other six, Landgraf said, just one other actually ended up seeing action.

"Yes, I can well imagine you saw 3 months of the worst type of hell. Nothing could be more miserable than Korea. Anyway, really was a hell hole, wasn't it?"

My Apology

While in S3, I got to be close friends with lot of the other enlisted men. One was a black soldier, Bob, who worked in personnel. Bob also had a bunk next to mine in the barracks. We became such good friends over a period of time where I never consciously thought of him as being of a different color. He was just a friend. We talked a lot about personal things in addition to work.

One day, out of the blue while we were talking, I said "nigger." Not even thinking. It just came out. I thought, *Oh, my God, I never wanted to do that.* I looked at him and said, "I apologize as much as it's possible for me to apologize.

"You know, you're a good friend of mine, and it's the last thing I wanted to do. And it just slipped because I've said it all my life."

And he said, "Well, you know, don't think anything of it. You and I have been good friends for a long time. The fact you didn't even think about when you said it really shows something about you not thinking colored or white."

If he was angry, he kept it well-hidden. In retrospect, I'm sure many black soldiers at the time let things slide when confronted with a racist remark. Our friendship went on like it had before, because I apologized and he was big enough to accept it.

Hot Springs

Off-base, some of my favorite places to relax were tea houses in the Japanese hot springs resort of Noboribetsu. They didn't serve much tea, instead mostly booze. I would go there with Don Davis and other buddies from Chitose I as often as possible. Noboribetsu was right up in the mountains. It was all very hill country, and it was also very Asian. They had modern things like streetlights and neon signs, but the streets weren't paved. Of course, our main interest was meeting girls. There were always a lot of young women around with names that ended with "ko," which means "child" in Japanese, such as Kimiko or Sachiko or Mariko.

The Japanese loved their hot springs and all the rituals of taking a bath in them. At one resort, they had a room with three holes in the floor that were about 3 or 4 feet deep, each containing hot water of increasing temperatures. The idea was for you to strip off all your clothes, wash yourself in cold water then get into the one that was least hot. Trust me. The least hot was hotter than any bath water I ever sat in during my life. But I found if I got in there slowly, kind of worked my way in, gradually the pain would ease and I could make it. Once I got acclimated it didn't seem that hot anymore. If I were being really brave, I'd go to the second one. The second one was hotter than hell at first, but if you sat there for a while it was okay. Well, I never dared go into the third one. It was just too painful.

I never went into the tubs during the day because there were too many people around, including women. I didn't want to meet any strangers in there. One night, another Army buddy and I decided to use the tubs when no one else was there. I eased my way naked into the least-hot one. He was in the next hottest.

Suddenly, along came three Japanese women. They proceeded to take off all their clothes, and then jump into the same tub I was in. They obviously were used to being naked around men they didn't know. In Japan, men and women didn't have two sets of bathrooms. It was the same with these hot baths.

As these women sat there, I wouldn't get out because I didn't want to stand up and expose myself. The women just talked to each other and ignored me, and I kind of looked off in the distance, turning into a very warm prune. After a while, they got up and went into the second tub. But I stayed right there. Eventually, they got up and dried off and put on their clothes and left. As soon as they were out the door, I popped out of there, dried off and got the hell out as fast as I could go, with my buddy not far behind.

Sometimes, I just liked to drive around and see the Japanese countryside. One day a group of us took a ride to the seashore, where we came upon this little town about 70 miles from our base. There weren't any other Americans around at all. I could tell right away we weren't welcome. There were none of the friendly faces we typically saw in Japan. Still, because we had driven all that distance, we went down to the shore to check out the ocean.

One Japanese fellow didn't say anything, but he glared like he was trying to start trouble. We didn't want any problems, so when it began to look like he was going to start a fight, we got back in our vehicle and went somewhere else. I suspect he was a Communist, because there were a lot of them around at that time. They even would have a Communist rally in Chitose every once in a while. On May 1, when Communists celebrated May Day, we were ordered not to go into town.

200 Little Orphan Girls

One day Captain Troy told me and some other soldiers that the local Catholic orphanage was looking for some men to do maintenance work. He asked us to gather volunteers. When five of us got there, we were greeted by the nuns running the place: one American from the Midwest, a European and a Japanese. Then we met the 200 little girls, all children of American soldiers and Japanese women. The children were absolutely sweet and adorable, but starved for attention. They quickly attached themselves to us, and us to them.

After our first trip to make repairs and do some painting around the orphanage, we looked for excuses to go back. There were about six or seven of us who did it on a regular basis.

My good friend Moose Terrgell in our office at S3 in Japan. He delighted the children by playing Santa at the local orphanage.

At Christmas, we took a collection on post and raised enough money to buy each little girl a dress, a ball, a doll and other little gifts. We also provided some turkeys and other food for the orphanage, and the nuns cooked dinner for us.

We loaded all the presents on a sled and towed it to the orphanage behind one of the jeeps. On the way there, another driver hit the sled with his car. He didn't damage any of the stuff, so we just loaded the presents into the other jeep and kept going.

One of our soldiers. Moose Terrgell, a great big guy, was made up like Santa Claus to give the gifts to the girls. The girls had never seen Santa before, and I'll never forget how sweet it was to watch their delighted faces.

On Easter, each of us picked out a girl and took her by bus to the post for an egg hunt. The girl I escorted, who was very lively, got so many eggs that some of the others were left with none. She sobbed and held on tightly to her eggs when the nuns suggested she share a few. Eventually, they convinced her to do so.

As a reward for giving all the help to the orphanage, Captain Troy gave the group of us permission to go off post for a day in a large Army truck. We decided to take a trip through snow-laden roads to a town about 40 miles north of our base. It was a Sunday afternoon and there wasn't a lot of traffic.

We got about five miles out of base when we skidded off the road into a deep ditch with a big snow bank. Nobody was hurt, but we were stuck. We tried pushing and pulling, using fence posts and everything, but we couldn't get that truck out.

We spotted a nearby farmhouse, which was actually just

wooden planks with a straw roof. We knocked and asked the owner if we could borrow his horse to help pull us out.

That's me on the right and U.S. soldier Jerry Dunahay, center, posing with the Japanese family that helped us get our truck pulled out of a ditch.

He was extremely pleasant and invited us inside to warm up. He then came out with a horse and hitched it to the back of the truck, and we pushed from the front and managed to get out of the ditch. We were relieved to get out, because otherwise we would have had to ask the Army to come after us, and we didn't want that. He invited us to stay for lunch, but we just gave him money to thank him.

Not long after we got back underway, we met a Japanese snowplow coming in the other direction. The road wasn't wide enough for our two big vehicles to pass. The plow driver had with him a policeman, who ordered us to back up. We knew, if we met a Japanese snowplow, it always had the right of way. So we had to back up about 2 1/2 miles to the nearest crossroad to pull off so he could get by.

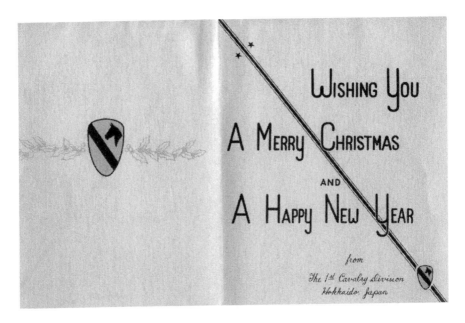

This is the official 1st Cavalry Christmas card, horse patch emblem and all, which I mailed from Japan to my parents in 1952.

.

Finally, we arrived at our destination and proceeded to the nearest little bar. We spent the next few hours getting acquainted with the young women there and having food and drink. We arrived back at the base late in the evening, happy indeed that we had a few hours away from military life.

As always, though, my family in Norwood was foremost in my mind, and Christmas 1952 was lonely without them. I typed and mailed this note just before the holidays.

> Dear Mom, Dad, Jean, Ronny and Joey,
>
> It is very difficult for me to buy anything suitable over here for you for Christmas and even more difficult to mail home. I thought it over and came up with an answer.

I want you to take two hundred dollars out of my bank account. It is to be used to help pay up any debts that you have. As for which debts, that is as you see fit.

I hope the kids won't be disappointed in not receiving individual presents but I think in the long run it will benefit them more than anything else.

With sincere wishes for the most Merry Christmas and Happy New Year; and with the silent prayer that I shall be home to share your next Christmas. I remain,

As ever,

God Bless You All.

Ken

CHAPTER 12: Homeward Bound

April 4, 1953

Dear Mom,

There are some more pictures for you to put away for me. There are also more on the way. I'm fine and hope this finds you the same. Only 97 more days to go.

Love,
Ken

By spring 1953, I was literally counting down the days until I won my discharge from the Army. I made no secret I couldn't wait to go home when my three years were up. However, that didn't stop Col. Bieri from calling me over to his desk when I didn't file paperwork to re-enlist.

"You've got a lot of smarts and very capable," he said in his fatherly way. "Why don't you want to stay in?"

To be honest, the main reason I was leaving is that I wanted to go home. I missed my family. I missed Norwood. But since he asked, I decided to give Col. Bieri a sense of my bitterness about how I had been treated in the Army.

"Sir," I began, "I have been overlooked repeatedly for promotions." I went on to explain how I had no unit to promote me while I studied at Fort Bliss, how the frozen rank in the Far East kept me stuck at PFC, and how the "acting corporal" designation and the resulting loss of pay seemed extremely unfair.

"Sir," I continued, "there are guys coming overseas as sergeants telling me what to do who don't have combat experience or anywhere near as much time in the service as I have. There are times they will come to me and ask what they should do, because I have more experience."

Col. Bieri quietly nodded his head.

"Well, corporal, that happens sometime in the Army, but sooner or later it irons itself out. I'll promise you one thing: If you stay in and re-enlist for another three years, I will personally see to it you will be a sergeant this July."

"Thank you, sir," I said, "But I want to go home."

The colonel took my refusal very well. Before I left, he wrote a very nice letter of thanks.

> 3 June 1953
>
> SUBJECT: Appreciation
> TO: Cpl. Kenneth LaRue
> RA12356511
>
> Upon your departure for the Zone of the Interior, may I take this opportunity to express to you my appreciation for your fine performance of duty in my section.

Your fine spirit, congenial attitude, ability to get each task done in a minimum of time, your soldierly bearing, resourcefulness and loyalty are qualities that will lead you to much success in civilian or other military endeavors.

I strongly urged you to make every effort to complete your schooling in your chosen work.

Leon Bieri
Lt. Col. Arty

I read his note with a little smile to myself. After his early grumbling about my uniform, I was amused by his reference to my "soldierly bearing."

Unfortunately, my soldierly bearing at that point also included a liberal use of a certain four-letter word that rolled out without much thought. My buddies and I had a cure for that. Whenever any of us got within 30 days of our scheduled discharge date, we gave him a brisk punch in the shoulder every time he used the F-word or any variation of it. We'd punch from about a foot away — enough to hurt without too much damage. After a few of those from buddies, I was cured of that word.

Back to Noboribetsu

By May 1953, I had about 90 days of leave accumulated. I held out hope that the Army would dismiss me a few weeks early, seeing that they were only going to pay me for 60 days of unused leave.

Not having much faith in Army math, I decided to use 10 of

those days on authorized leave at my favorite hot spot: Noboribetsu. It only cost me 10 cents each to go there by train and another $5 to stay for the week in the Grand Hotel. The food and beer were extra, but even they were inexpensive.

A view from a hotel room in Noboribetsu, Japan, during one of my visits to the hot springs there.

Don "Chibi" Davis and I arrived there on May 26. Like all these places, the bar girls at the Grand Hotel were quite attractive and friendly. Don was a nice-looking guy with blonde hair and very pale complexion. The Japanese girls just loved him.

For a couple of days, we spent our time boozing in the bars and soaking in the hot tubs, and occasionally getting out to explore the village of Noboribetsu.

On the third afternoon, unbeknownst to me at the time, orders came through at headquarters for my immediate discharge.

My buddies saw them and went to a captain in my office. Unfortunately, it was the same captain who never liked me because I wouldn't do his paperwork ahead of higher-ranking officers. So he just blew them off when my friends asked if they could go get me.

"The hell with him," he said, my buddies told me later. "If he wanted to go so badly, he should have been here."

Fortunately, my pals didn't let it rest. They went over his head to Col. Bieri.

"What?" the colonel said when told my discharge came through. "I am giving you an order right now: You go get him."

And just then General Cooper came to his office doorway. He overheard the conversation. He said, "What's more, you make out the paperwork to go off the mainline route to get there quicker, and I'll sign it."

A couple of my friends left in a jeep and arrived at the hot springs at night, dressed with MP arm bands, even though they weren't with the military police. I was sitting in a bar with Don and a couple of Japanese girls when they showed up.

"Okay, LaRue, you've had it," one barked in an MP sort of way.

"What the hell are you talking about? Why are you guys all the way up here?" I asked.

"Do you want to go home or do you want to stay here?"

"I want to go home."

"Well, you better get your ass back to the barracks, because the orders came through for you to leave in the morning." I paused only long enough to grab my duffel bag and say goodbye to Don.

I got back to the base about 10 p.m. and immediately began packing. The next morning, on little or no sleep, I proceeded to "clear post," which consisted of getting every department to sign off that I didn't have any outstanding debts.

I did all this while riding in style. General Cooper sent his driver to pick me up and drive me around post to clear. The driver just had to remove the red plate on the front with the general's gold star. Even so, my buddies were impressed when I pulled up in the general's personal means of transportation with a chauffeur.

Everything happened so fast I barely had time to say goodbye to my buddies. I had no time at all to write a detailed letter to my folks.

However, the guys in the Artillery Headquarters put together this comedic form letter mailed to parents of those of us returning home. The letter offered tongue-in-cheek advice to "look with indulgence" on any of my possible new habits, such as sleeping on the floor and having bath water set at 120 degrees. It added about my return to the U.S., "Remember that he is in a strange land, where people don't take baths in big pools in public, where they don't suffer broken bones in boarding a train, and where the women don't all have black hair, slant eyes, bow legs and are not all five feet tall."

In Hakodate, I boarded the Toya Maru, this huge train ferry, to make the trip to the main island of Honshu, about three or four hours across the water. The ferry ride was uneventful for me, but about a year later this same ferry sank in a storm with the loss of 1,153 lives, including 35 from the 1st Cavalry Division.

As our train took me past Tokyo, it suddenly halted. Word came down that the train had hit a man who was drunk and had staggered onto the tracks. They had to clean up the mess before they could take us the rest of the way.

Is That Bieri?

I returned to Camp Drake for three days of processing, including required inoculations before traveling back to the United States. Then I boarded the USNS General Simon B. Buckner, a transport ship sailing for Seattle that was named after one of the highest-ranking Americans killed during World War II.

The Buckner was a slightly smaller ship than the General Meigs that transported me to Japan in 1951. The officers and men with Japanese brides were housed on the upper deck and the rest of us on the lower part.

I looked up at one point – and there was the Col. Bieri, heading back to the States with the rest of us. I thought: *Son of gun!* The colonel promised to personally ensure I would be promoted to sergeant if I re-enlisted, but it turns out the Hokkaido Bear wasn't going to be there to do so. Later I learned from my buddies still back at Artillery Headquarters that Bieri had transferred out right after me and was replaced by another colonel.

Sailing on the Buckner, I really didn't have a hell of a lot to do.

Because I was experienced in the service, I knew to stay out of sight until they chose all the Army people to help clean up and do other tasks on the ship.

I took time to write.

June 11, 1953

Dear Mom, Dad, Jean, Ronny and Joe,

By the time you read this letter, I will probably be on my way across the States, bound for Camp Kilmer. You probably wonder why I haven't written at least to say I was leaving. When my orders came to ship out, I was on 10 days leave in Noboribetsu hot springs resort in southern Hokkaido. Two of my buddies drove up after me at 10 o'clock at night so I could I make the shipment at noon the next day.

At this writing, I'm aboard the U.S.S. General Buckner two days out of Yokohama and scheduled to arrive in Seattle on the 19th of June. I will stay in Seattle 1 1/2 to two days and then go to Camp Kilmer in New Jersey for discharge. I will write again when I get there.

It was awfully hard to say goodbye to Hokkaido. I left a lot of friends and many good times behind.

I have three boxes on the way home. When they arrive, please do not open them. Just put them away somewhere and I will open them when I get home.

In another nine more days, I will be in the States. It doesn't seem possible after all these months that I'm really going home. In just 38 days I will be home with all of you again.

I don't know how long I will be in Camp Kilmer before discharge. I should arrive there around June 24. I have 71 days furlough time coming, so they may discharge me early. I don't know.

I will mail this letter as soon as possible after I arrive in Seattle.

The reason I ask you to put the three boxes away until I arrive home is because I have some personal things in the boxes, and the rest of it I want to take care of myself.

Today is the 15th of June, Monday. Tomorrow is also the 15th of June, Monday. That's because we will cross the International Date Line shortly. We lost a day coming from Seattle to Yokohama, and now we're gaining it back on the return trip.

I'm writing with my new Parker 21 pen, which I purchased at the ship's PX. It was only $3. At the regular PX, it would cost $5-$8 and in the civilian market probably around $12-$15.

On my long, tiring journey back home, I'm carrying 12 Japanese recordings. So far, none have been broken. If my luck holds up for a while longer, I shall have them safely across the

States and soon home.

The past few days, all I have been thinking about is the States and home. Last night, I started thinking about the macaroni and tomato we used to have for chow when Dad was at work. I got so hung up thinking about it that my stomach ached. That is one dish I don't remember eating in my three years in the Army.

I've got many pictures and souvenirs and so on that I have picked up since I have been here to show you when I get home. I imagine there is plenty at home for me to see.

It has been a long time, but it's nearly at an end. Some of these mornings I shall awaken to find that I'm a civilian again. That will be great.

I don't believe I shall ever regret the fact I enlisted when I did. By enlisting when I did and not waiting nine months, I missed all the reserve obligations. In other words, I will have a complete discharge and no reserve to serve, whereas most of the other fellows who came in later have the regular enlistment plus a number of years of reserve.

We're supposed to arrive in Seattle on the 19th or 20th of June. I will mail this letter as soon as possible after we arrive. As it only takes 1 and 1/2 days to process in Seattle, I should probably be on my way across the U.S. by the same you receive this letter. I will drop you a line as soon as possible as I arrive in Camp Kilmer so as to let you know where I am.

I will close now, wishing you the best of everything always.

See you soon.

Love,

Ken

Good, Clean Fun in Seattle

The ship sailed up the Puget Sound on June 19. On the way in, we watched a couple of guys drunker than a skunk clowning in a fishing boat. Once in a while one guy got so tipsy he fell overboard, and the other guy had to swing around and pick him up. Eventually, we realized it was all just entertainment for our benefit, but they kept us laughing for quite a while.

If that wasn't enough, there were a group of can-can girls dancing on the docks, just some sweet high school and college girls entertaining the troops. Later, I read that the Ladies Aid Society of Seattle wanted to ban their performance, saying all those lifted skirts weren't good for our morals. I wondered what they would say if they had seen some performances in the dance balls of Hokkaido.

There was a professional photographer who took pictures all up and down the ship. There is a photo of me looking over the railing, absolutely thrilled to be in the United States after being gone for two years. You can easily find me in the photo because I'm the only one in a white hat. Our unit happened to switch early to uniforms known as "suntans" while most of the other guys were in olive drabs worn in the winter.

That's me in the white hat as the USNS General Simon B. Buckner docks in Seattle.

I was transported from there back to Fort Lawton for processing and some of the best food I had tasted in a long time. We even had fresh milk, which wasn't available overseas, where I could only get powdered milk.

After I was assigned barracks, I was shown to the banks of telephones where I could call home. It had been a long, long time since I talked to anybody from my family. It was 1 in the morning Norwood time when Mom answered the phone and, despite the late hour, everyone got up to listen.

To my surprise, they knew I was on my way home. That day's

Watertown Daily Times carried a short story revealing that "Cpl. Kenneth LaRue of Norwood arrived in Seattle, Washington, on his way for discharge." One of our neighbor ladies was so excited she came running right down to the house and showed my mother the newspaper.

A day or so later, the Army loaded me and 34 other enlisted men who served in the Far East on a C-47 civilian plane scheduled to take us to Philadelphia, where we could be bused to nearby Camp Kilmer for discharge. There was also a colonel aboard. We made one stop in Cheyenne, Wyoming, then took off again. I was soon asleep.

I woke up in mid-flight because I felt the change of air pressure in my ears. I looked up to see one of the two pilots leaning over me. He was pointing a flashlight out the window toward a propeller.

"What's the matter?" I asked.

"Nothing to worry about," he said as he walked back to the cockpit.

I looked out the window. I was shocked to see we couldn't have been 200 feet off the flat Kansas prairie. Eventually, I saw people running out of their houses, looking up at us, probably wondering what the hell was going on.

We flew and flew and flew like that. I began to wonder: *Are we going to crash?* Because the plane didn't fly any higher.

All of a sudden, the plane kind of banked and there was a runway right ahead of us. We landed in Kansas City, Kansas.

The plane had some sort of mechanical problem, and there were no immediate repairs or replacements in store for most of us. The colonel flew out immediately on some other plane. The Army loaded the enlisted men on buses and took us to a hotel in Kansas City, Missouri, just across the river. We were told that's where all the stewardesses stayed, so the guys were pretty happy about that. The next day, our airplane's engine troubles prompted a short report in the local newspaper, which kind of made us feel like celebrities.

The Army paid for our hotel and meals. I wired home for a little money from Mom, who took 30 bucks or something out of my account so I would have some money to party a little bit. We did. We partied. We didn't see many stewardesses, but we saw a lot of young women and they saw us.

On the third day, we took off again and finally landed in Philadelphia, probably around 3 in the morning. The Army took us by bus into Camp Kilmer for the discharge process.

"We can do this one of two ways," an officer told us. "It's late and I know you didn't have much sleep. We can start processing today and you'll be out three days from now, or you rest today and start processing tomorrow and you can be out in four days."

To a man, we all said the same thing: "Start today. We'll do without the rest."

On the third day at Camp Kilmer, a bus pulled up waiting to take us to a building where we would get our discharge papers. We were all standing there, dressed in our clean uniforms, when these privates came up and ordered us to clean the barracks where we stayed. Most of us were sergeants or master sergeants or corporals who were minutes from exiting the Army. Now suddenly a bunch of privates were telling us what to do, and apparently they had been given authority to do so.

Our sense of discipline wasn't terribly strong at that point. A lot of us cleaned up by stuffing our junk inside rolled mattresses on the beds.

We thought we were done when a private came over, pointed to me and three others, and ordered us to go to the mess hall and help to serve chow.

"Pick out some guys who aren't going to be discharged today," said a master sergeant among us. "Let them do it. We've got our clean uniforms on."

The private stared back. "That's an order. You go over there or I will get a hold of the lieutenant and you won't be going home today."

We headed to the mess hall, angry as hell but not taking chances at spending a day longer in the Army than need be. We started scooping chow onto trays when this master sergeant among us threw down his spoon.

"I've had enough of this shit," he said. He stalked over to the captain's office. He knew officers all respect a master sergeant because he's been in the service a long time.

When the sergeant explained we were ordered to serve chow, the captain sighed: "They weren't supposed to do that," he said of the order from the privates. "What the hell is the matter with them?"

The captain immediately sent over some of his enlisted men to relieve every one of us along the line.

Triumphantly, we returned to the barracks. The pisser of a private was furious by then, because we had showed him up with an officer. But he didn't do anything more while we all filed outside again, ready to board the bus.

"Nobody load on the bus yet," he announced then. "Just stand there."

He went back into the barracks and started unrolling all those mattresses, throwing all this garbage on the floor we had stuffed in there. He apparently had seen soldiers do this before.

Then he walked back out with another order: "You guys left a big mess in the barracks. Clean it up."

For the next 15 or 20 minutes, we did two things: We picked up garbage thrown on the floor from our mattresses and we fantasized what we would do to a certain private if we could get him alone.

We finally got onto that bus and on our way to the discharge center. Someone handed me final release papers and back pay. I had $320 coming. I immediately went to the PX and bought myself a wristwatch, because I knew it would be the last time in a long while that I would be able to afford a nice one.

My official date of discharge was June 26, 1953, almost three years to the day after the start of the Korean War.

I expected to wait for a bus heading north, but one of the other soldiers – a guy I never met before – was from Binghamton, New York, and his parents were there to pick him up. He asked if anyone wanted a ride north. Since Binghamton was on my way to Syracuse, I jumped at the chance.

His mom and dad were the nicest people in the world, and they were so happy to see their boy home. His mom kept turning to me and saying, "You want to make sure you write us now."

"Mom, we don't even know each other," her son explained.

She just couldn't understand that. Every few miles she'd turn to me and say something like, "You want to make sure you write to us." After a while, I just nodded.

In Binghamton, they dropped me off at the bus station, and I got to Syracuse that night. By then it was too late to get a bus north, so I checked into the Hotel Yates, back where I stayed three years earlier.

The first thing in the morning I boarded a bus heading for Norwood. Before I got half-way there, the bus broke down. We waited an hour or two for a replacement bus. But this one was only going as far as Potsdam. So when it arrived there, I had to take a cab to Norwood. I stopped at Rat Wilkins restaurant, where the buses came in and I expected to meet my family.

"Your father was here earlier, but he left when the bus didn't show up," someone told me as I looked around the restaurant.

I called Slim Robinson, the cab driver in the village for almost forever. He was thrilled to offer me a ride home. He loved taking some kid home who had been in the service. When we got to Elm Street, he even helped bring my bags to the door.

"I brought your kid home," he announced when the door opened.

More than 50 years later, I get choked up thinking about that moment. The joy I felt is hard to describe. Everyone rushed over to greet me. I remember the chatter of my siblings, the warm hugs of my mom, the misty eyes of my Dad and my own quiet relief of being home for good.

And then, except for one major instance, the Korean War and Army life in general quickly became a distant memory.

CHAPTER 13: The Forgotten War

I got a call in April 1955 from the parents of high school classmate Bobby Cutler. They told me the Army had confirmed what everyone feared since he was declared missing in action in 1951: Bobby was dead. The Army had finally recovered his remains, officially identified them, and was now returning them to his family for burial. The parents asked me to be a pall bearer at his funeral.

By then I had pretty much put any Army thoughts behind me. Just a month or so after I was discharged, an armistice was signed that ended the fighting in Korea, and it seemed our whole country was happy to move on from the war. There were no big celebrations for our veterans like the kind when World War II ended.

I carry my wife, Carol, on our wedding day in 1954.

I began dating Carol LaPlante just a few months after I got out of the service. I attended college for a while, then dropped out to get married to Carol in May 1954. My first son,

Robert, was born in March 1955. (He was named after my cousin and childhood best friend Bob Christian.) I never repaired any more radars, but the clerical experience in the Army was valuable: I landed an office job at the Raquette River Paper Mill in Potsdam.

At first after I got home from the war, I might go to a bar and have a few beers with some of the guys who had been in Korea. We'd talk about it a little bit, just among ourselves. After all the stories were told and re-told, that wasn't fun anymore.

I corresponded for a while with several of my Army buddies. In 1953, I got a Christmas card from 1st Cavalry drinking buddy Moose Terrgell, who was out of the Army and now in the air conditioning business.

"Hi, Candy," Moose wrote, "I sure was surprised to get your card yesterday. This Christmas is sure different from the way we spent the last one at the orphanage. Hope the kids have it half as good this year as when we gave the party."

Around the same time, I got a letter from the parents of Ralph James, the radar school buddy with whom I spent the ship ride to Japan playing cards. His parents told me that Ralph died in the hospital about a week after we parted at Camp Drake. I don't know if he had a heart attack or what. His parents wrote to ask what I knew about his final days. I wrote back and said he was a very good friend of mine. I told them everything I could remember about him at Fort Bliss and during the voyage over. They invited me to visit them in New Mexico, but by then I didn't have money for that kind of travel.

The call from Bobby Cutler's parents brought me back into

one last Army duty. I learned then that he was killed May 18, 1951, while fighting with the 38th Infantry Regiment, 2nd Infantry Division, during a battle in South Korea.

All six pall bearers at his funeral May 2, 1955, at St. Andrew's Church were military veterans from Norwood who had been in the service at the same time. They included my old friend Punchy Palmer. The funeral had all the military touches provided by the American Legion post in Norwood.

ROBERT CUTLER "CUTTY"
"YOU MAY CHARGE HIM WITH MURDER
—OR WANT OF SENSE—BUT THE
SLIGHTEST APPROACH TO A FALSE PRE-
TENSE WAS NEVER AMONG HIS CRIMES."
ACTIVITIES: J. V. BASKETBALL 1 YR.,
CROSS COUNTRY 1 YR., TRACK 1 YR.,
VOLLEYBALL 1 YR., CLASS OFFICER 1
YR., SENIOR PLAY, INTRAMURALS.

My classmate Bobby Cutler is seen in my Norwood High School 1950 yearbook.

Bobby's mother, of course, was devastated by his death, but she told me she finally was at peace knowing his body was home and that he wasn't suffering in some North Korean prison camp.

The Story of Fox Company

After the armistice, I finally learned the story of what happened to Fox Company on Thanksgiving Eve and Thanksgiving 1951, when most of the platoon led by Lt. James L. Stone had been wiped out. In interviews since, Stone recalled that trouble began when the enemy began shooting white phosphorus shells in anticipation of a probable assault. Around 9 p.m., the Chinese launched a major artillery and mortar attack.

Stone radioed for the Army to shoot flares high in the sky. With parts of valley illuminated, he saw two battalions of enemy troops – approximately 800 men -- racing up the hill to attack his isolated outpost of 48 soldiers.

Over the next three hours, those men in Fox Company repelled six enemy attacks, with many dead or wounded on both sides. About 1 a.m., Stone thought the outpost had held when suddenly the Chinese threw another battalion at his platoon.

Stone moved calmly among the men, despite enemy fire, as he urged them to "make every shot count." At one point, when a flamethrower stopped working, Stone fixed it then handed it to a soldier.

Eventually the fighting turned to hand-to-hand combat. At times Stone had to knife the enemy with his bayonet. He was wounded three times, including by a bullet that pierced his throat and came out the back of his neck. One of the soldiers saved Stone's life by putting a bandage over that neck wound.

Stone and the other survivors from Fox Company were taken

prisoner after they ran out of ammunition. Some died in the prison camp. Stone credited part of his survival to the fact he was an officer and the Chinese hoped to gain information, which he said they never did. He spent 22 months as a POW until he was released in a prisoner exchange Oct. 27, 1953. That's when the public learned that he had been selected to receive the Medal of Honor

I never met Stone, but I've read a lot about him because he is very active in 1st Cavalry veterans groups, helping to keep the heroic story of Fox Company alive.

We are among an ever-shrinking group of Korean War veterans. We are old men now, those of us who survive. I learned a few years ago that my squad leader and good friend, Steve Babcock, had died of a heart attack.

Our Past in Ashes

In 2005, I sent away for a copy of my medical records, hoping I might be a lucky one whose records survived a July 12, 1973, fire at the National Personnel Records Center. I got a form letter back from the Personnel Records Center telling me the requested records were "not in our files." It noted than most Army personnel records from 1912 to 1959 were destroyed in the fire. Details of my back problems during Army service apparently survive only in my memories.

I also destroyed many old photos and letters involving women I knew, including some from Japan. Before I got married, I wanted to make a clear break from my romantic past. In the 1950s, my parents had behind their house a burn barrel, which I used to destroy at least 100 pictures. Ronny and Joe were just young fellows then, and they were hoping I would drop one on the ground so they could get it and run off and show my father. But one by one I dropped each photo into the fire. Then I ran a stick in there and twirled it to make sure there was nothing left but ashes before I left.

I packed away the rest of the letters and photos and documents and went on with my life. Once in a while I'd pull out this big black book, "First Cavalry Division, Korea, June 1950 to January 1952." I'd go thumb through it and look at the listing of George Company soldiers in the back, refreshing my memory of guys I served with in Korea.

To this day, though, I haven't read many books about the Korean War or viewed many movies about it. I did see "Bridges of Toko-Ri" with William Holden and "Jet Pilot" with John Wayne. I saw "The Steel Helmet" with Gene Evans.

However, I have never gotten around to seeing the most famous movie about the Korean War: "Pork Chop Hill," starring Gregory Peck. Trailers for the 1959 film made it seem a bit too realistic for my tastes, although I never knew until very recently that Pork Chop Hill was the same place where we had our outpost.

My Thoughts About 'M*A*S*H'

Then in the early 1970s came the TV series "M*A*S*H." I never saw the earlier movie version, but I watched the TV series because it could be really funny, with Radar O'Reilly and Hot Lips Houlihan and all the gang. It really did look like Korea, especially the hills. The helicopters were just like the ones we had in Korea.

I know the series was really meant as a barely disguised

commentary on the Vietnam War. However, by setting it during the Korean War, the only real casualty was the truth. If you saw that show and didn't know better, you'd believe all the American medical teams were anti-American and pro-North Korean, and that the North Koreans were really nice people and wouldn't hurt a soul. When those North Koreans came in wounded, our doctors would treat them with a great deal of respect, because they were nice guys. All that baloney was because of liberal series star Alan Alda and some of the writers.

I thought, *I went over to Korea and risked my life in combat, and now some Hollywood hot shot is trying to do a version of the war that isn't true at all.*

Of course, "M*A*S*H" was comedy entertainment. It also did help lift the Korean War from being forgotten, although it was still overshadowed by Vietnam and especially World War II. In fact, while I can count on one hand the books I've read about the Korean War, I've read literally hundreds on World War II, and watched lots of movies about that war such as "Saving Private Ryan," and TV miniseries such as "Band of Brothers."

World War II was exceptionally clear as a battle between good and evil. Hitler and his Nazi Germans were such cruel bastards. Everyone knew that. When the war ended, and when we saw what they did to the Jews in the concentration camps, we learned that wartime horror stories about them were even worse than we imagined.

We knew from the start of World War II just how evil the Japanese could be due to their attack on Pearl Harbor and their brutal treatment during occupations of China and other countries. Their leaders insisted their own people fight to the death. I grew very fond of many Japanese people and feel bad so many citizens suffered because of their evil leadership. However, I'm convinced, as many others are, that we would have lost thousands and thousands of our men, and maybe millions of Japanese, if we hadn't used the atom bomb to force them to surrender.

I became interested in World War II while in Japan. Our headquarters building had a small library with books on several World War II battles and various tactics. I would go in there and pick up a book and get started on it and, boy, I'd stay with it until I was done with the whole thing because it was very, very interesting.

When I got home it was just a natural thing that I was going to continue to read books on World War II. Maybe a lot of the appeal was that I was too young to fight that war and never experienced its horrors first-hand. It is also a much clearer story of the good guys vs. the bad guys.

To Err Is Truman

As for fighting in Korea, our leaders didn't even want to call it a war. A lot of veterans never got over their anger with President Harry Truman for calling the Korean War a "police action." He was wrong. It was just as much a blood-drenched war as any other. In some cases, it was worse. As far as I'm concerned, it was war.

It's since gotten the nickname "The Forgotten War." I think most Americans didn't want to remember it because, unlike World War II, we did not achieve unconditional surrender or total victory. It was the first war where we almost got our tails clipped. We didn't. We pushed the North Koreans and

Chinese out of South Korea, and that's why the South to this day remains a democracy. On the other hand, we didn't bring democracy to North Korea. The saddest fact is that an estimated 1.2 million people were killed and millions more wounded in a senseless civil war.

The older I have gotten, the prouder I have become of my military service. I served with what I think was distinction. I wasn't a hero. On the other hand, I wasn't a coward, either. I fought alongside the other guys. I did my duty.

I don't think any of us who fought there wanted it to be a forgotten war. People like Steve Babcock and James L. Stone* were among the thousands of Army soldiers who risked their lives to fight for democracy and freedom and to serve our country, just as soldiers have done in many other wars. In Korea, many such as Bobby Cutler gave up their lives or were wounded in that quest.

We hoped – and I still hope – these sacrifices will never be forgotten.

*W.L. note: James L. Stone, who reached the rank of colonel before retiring from the Army in 1980, died November 9, 2012, exactly three weeks before my dad passed away. I don't believe my father knew about this loss of a fellow veteran.

About the Authors

Kenneth LaRue shows souvenirs from his Army days to his son, William, over the kitchen table in 2005.

Kenneth J. LaRue is the recipient of several awards and decorations for his Army service from 1951-1953, including the Combat Infantry Badge, Korean Campaign Ribbon with two bronze stars, United Nations Ribbon and Japan Occupation Ribbon. He worked for the Unionville paper mill from 1954 to 1974, and was employed as the Potsdam village clerk from 1975 to 1994. He and his wife, the former Carol LaPlante, had three children and four grandchildren. Their marriage ended in divorce. Ken was a member of the Canton VFW; a facilitator of the Divorced and Separated Support

Group at St. Mary's Church in Potsdam; and was a founding member of the local Solo Singles group. He died November 30, 2012, after a long illness.

William D. LaRue, married father of two, is an award-winning journalist, former TV critic for The Post-Standard in Syracuse, and a website producer for several major newspapers. Bill once owned one of the world's largest collections of licensed merchandise from the TV series "The Simpsons." He is author of the 1999 book "Collecting Simpsons!"

Made in the USA
Middletown, DE
29 December 2015